# REDISCOVERING PHOTOGRAPHY

# REDISCOVERING PHOTOGRAPHY

by Eugene F. Provenzo, Jr.
and Asterie Baker Provenzo

designs and illustrations by
Peter A. Zorn, Jr.

OAK TREE PUBLICATIONS, INC.
PUBLISHERS, LA JOLLA, CALIFORNIA

First Edition
Manufactured in the United States of America
For information write to: Oak Tree Publications, Inc.
P.O. Box 1012, La Jolla, CA 92038

**Library of Congress Cataloging in Publication Data**

Provenzo, Eugene F
    Rediscovering photography.

    (Young inventor series; 1)
    SUMMARY:  Discusses the history of the camera, the development of photography, and the scientists, inventors, and photographers who made important contributions. Includes experiments.
    1.  Photography—Juvenile literature.  [1.  Photography]  I.  Provenzo, Asterie Baker, joint author.  II.  Zorn, Peter A.  III.  Title.  IV.  Series.
TR149.P76      770      80-17769
ISBN 0-916392-55-4

All experiments in this book are completely safe when properly conducted. However, some may require more caution than others. The publisher and authors have carefully detailed the necessary precautions that should be taken, and encourage the readers to fully understand all experiments prior to conducting them in order to better understand the specific phenomenon and to avoid any unnecessary mishap.

1 2 3 4 5 6 7 8 9    84 83 82 81 80

FOR TERRY, GENE, REE AND CHARLIE —
THANKS FOR PUTTING US IN THE PICTURE.

# Table of Contents to Experiments

# ACKNOWLEDGMENTS

Our thanks go to the many people who have helped make REDISCOVERING PHOTOGRAPHY possible. Important assistance in assembling the visual materials for this book was provided by the staff of the National Archives, the Library of Congress and the George Eastman House. Helen Beibel, Mildred Merrick and Patricia Pardo of Richter Library, University of Miami, were particularly helpful in ordering special materials and encouraging us in our research. Dr. Robert Hendricks and Dr. Lennie Middleton, School of Education and Allied Professions, University of Miami; George Chillag, Broward Community College; Roy W. Carpenter and Ruth Dye, Communication Services, University of Miami; Stephen Fuller of Miami and Al Rothfarb, Dade County Public Schools, were particularly helpful with technical suggestions and assistance. Elizabeth Lasensky of Miami provided invaluable help in researching the book. Dr. Scott Baldwin of the Department of Educational Psychology, University of Miami, was kind enough to take time from a busy schedule to check the readability of the text. As always, our thanks go to Ann and Steven Freedman for their encouragement and support for our work. We would also like to thank Joanne Walker for first introducing us to photography, and Steve Shore, Peter Zorn and Julia Thrane for tolerating endless technical questions.

**REDISCOVERING PHOTOGRAPHY** is a book about the inventions that have made photography what it is today. It is also a book about people who have played an important part in the history of photography: scientists, inventors, artists and photographers.

Throughout this book you will be able to experiment and re-create many of these inventions just as they were done over the past 1,000 years! As the Swiss psychologist Jean Piaget has explained, "The essential functions of intelligence consist in understanding and inventing, in other words, in building up structures by structuring reality."

You will be able to "rediscover photography" for yourself by making your own **camera** obscura, pinhole camera, telephoto camera and even a camera able to take wide-angle pictures. You will also be able to make sunprints and negative and positive photographic prints.

Many of the experiments and inventions in this book can be made with things found around your home. Some of the experiments will require materials you have to buy at a photography store. Complete, easy-to-follow instructions and diagrams are given for all of the experiments you will be doing. And patterns are included for all the inventions and cameras you will be making.

Once you have finished reading REDISCOVERING PHOTOGRAPHY, you will have discovered the people, the great experiments, cameras and photographs that have made photography the science and art it is today. You will also discover how photography has given us new ways of looking at the world and universe we live in.

**CAMERA**
**A camera is a closed box with a hole in one end and a piece of film or a photographic plate in the other. Light enters the box through the hole and strikes the chemically prepared surface of the film or plate to form the image.**

## LENS

The lens focuses the rays of light from the object and projects them (reversed or upside-down) onto the film.

## DIAPHRAGM

A mechanism, usually made of overlapping pieces of metal, which is used to control the amount of light that strikes the film.

## FOCAL PLANE SHUTTER

A movable, protective shield in front of the focal plane which is used to protect the film from light.

## FILM

The film receives the image on its chemically treated surface and records it.

## FILM ADVANCE

Winds the film from one spool to another, if the camera uses roll film or cartridges.

## VIEWING SYSTEM

The mechanism you look through to see and focus the object or subject you are photographing.

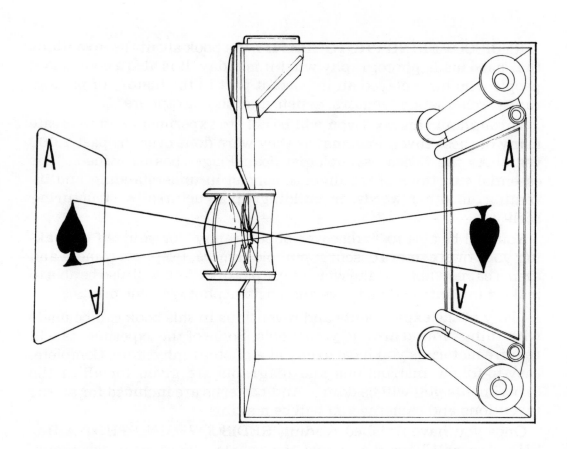

Most people think that photography was invented in the 1800s. The science of photography, or the ability to make permanent images by using chemically treated glass or paper, is a relatively new discovery. But many of the scientific principles that make photography possible have been known for a much longer time.

In fact, long before the first picture camera was invented, the mechanism for photography was known to exist in nature. Our eyes and the eyes of most animals operate like a camera.

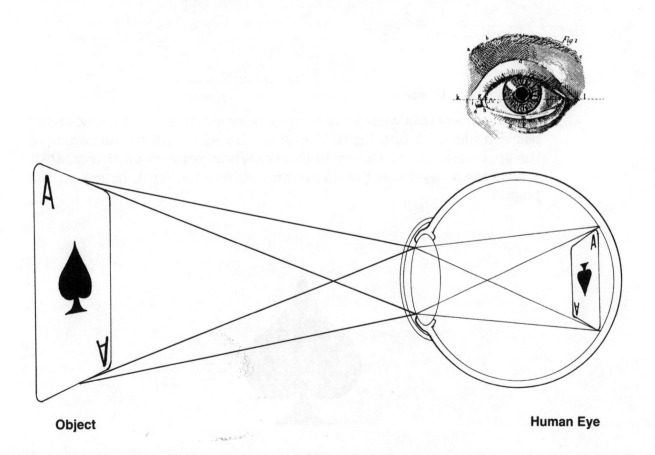

**Object**

**Human Eye**

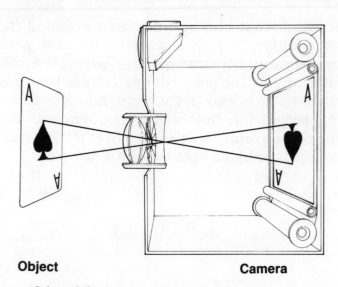

**Object**                    **Camera**

You can see this with your own eyes by staring at the black spade below under a strong light. Focus on the white dot in the center of the spade and count slowly to thirty. When your reach thirty, shift your eyes away from the spade and stare at a blank space on the page.

What you should see is a reverse image of the black spade, or a white spade, in the blank space. When you stared at the black spade, the image was recorded on the retina in each of your eyes. It takes the retina a while to chemically recharge and be able to receive a new image. Therefore, the image of the black spade remained and appeared as a white spade even when you were actually staring at a blank white space!

The retina is a delicate, light-sensitive membrane located in the back of the eye. It is connected by the optic nerve to the brain. Like the film in a camera, the retina receives the image or picture projected by the lens of the eye.

Both your eye and a camera need a lens to focus the rays of light that bounce off the object. When light hits the object, it bounces off in all directions. These rays would hit your eye, just as they would hit the film in a camera, in a mixed-up jumble that would appear to be a big blur instead of the image of the object. The lens is necessary to control and direct the light rays where they belong to form the image of the object.

The explanation for the inverted image is quite simple. Light travels in straight lines. The rays of light reflected from the bottom of an image will travel through the lens in the eye and continue in a straight line to the top of the retina. In the same way, the rays of light reflected from the top of the object will enter the lens of the eye and travel toward the bottom of the retina. The optic nerve transmits the upside-down image from the retina to your brain where it is inverted so that what you see is actually right-side-up.

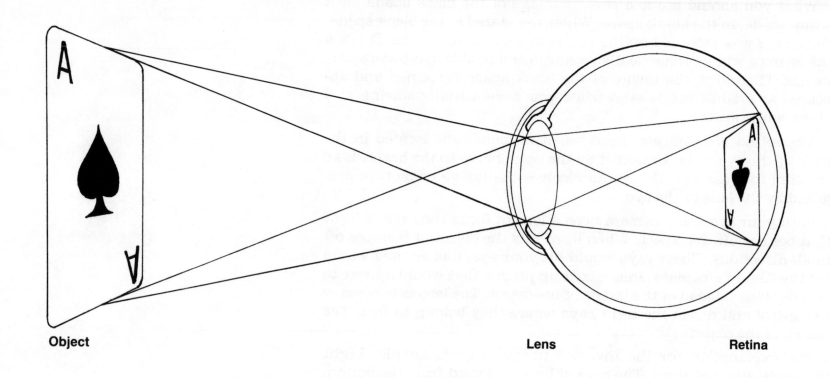

**Object**

**Lens**

**Retina**

**OPTICS**
**The scientific study of light and vision.**

This scientific principle became the first important step in the discovery of photography. In the 900s, the Arab mathematician and scientist, Alhazen of Basara, wrote a book on **optics.** In his work, Alhazen explained that when light was let through a small hole in a tent or darkened room, an upside-down or inverted image of what was outside would be projected on the wall. Those objects which were light-colored reflected a lot of light when projected through the hole. Those that were darker, reflected little or no light. This princi-

16

ple became the basis for a device known as the **camera obscura,** which actually means "a darkened room" in Latin.

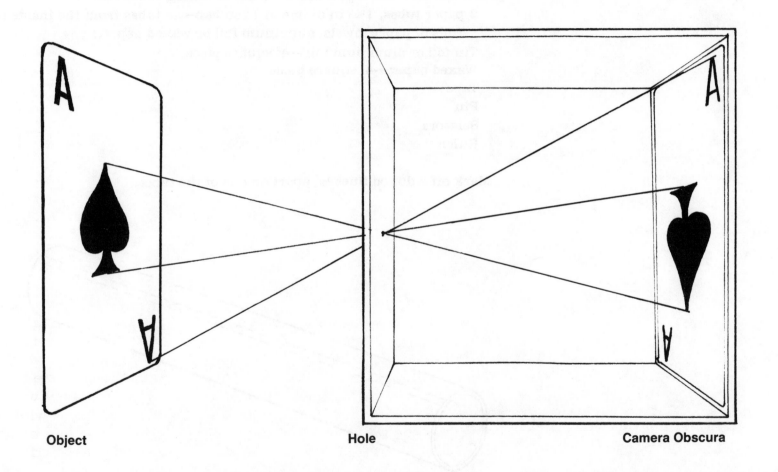

Object · Hole · Camera Obscura

You can best see how a camera obscura works by making a simple one of your own. To make it you will need the following materials:

2 paper tubes, 1½″ in diameter (You can use tubes from the inside of rolls of paper towels, aluminum foil or waxed paper.)

Tin foil or aluminum foil—4″ square piece

Waxed paper—4″ square piece

Tape

Pin

Scissors

Ruler

Mark off 2 dotted lines ⅛″ apart on one of the tubes.

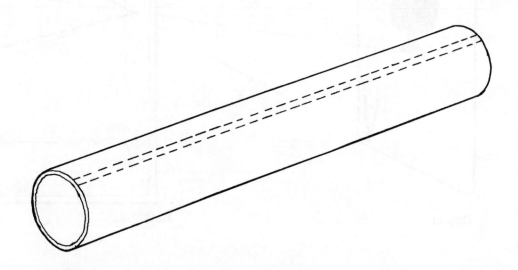

Cut a ⅛″ strip out of the tube, along the dotted lines, with the scissors.

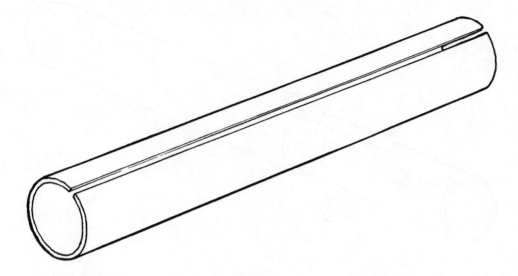

Compress the tube and tape it together.

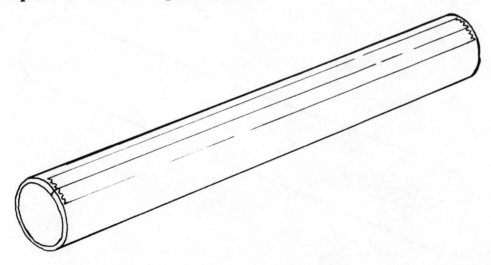

**The smaller tube should now slide back and forth inside the larger tube.**

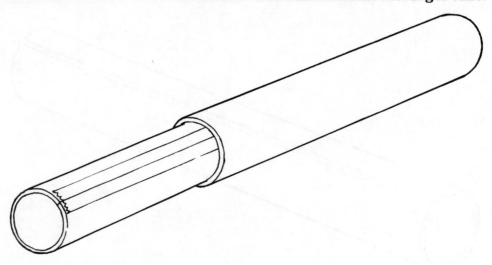

**Tape the tinfoil over the end of the larger tube as shown.**

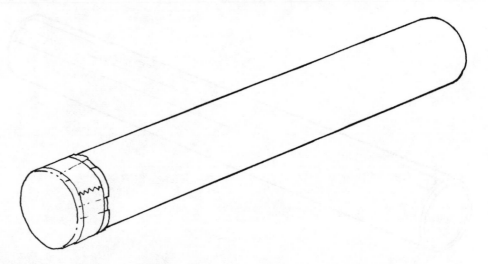

Punch a hole with the pin in the center of the tinfoil.

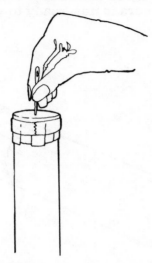

Now cover the end of the smaller tube with waxed paper and tape it as shown.

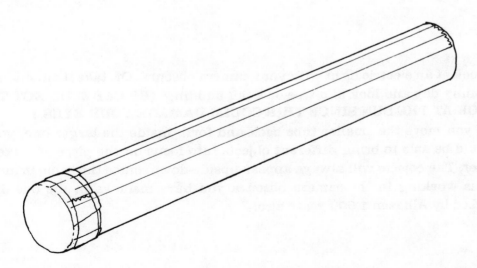

Insert the waxed paper end of the small tube into the open end of the larger tube. Your camera obscura is now ready to use.

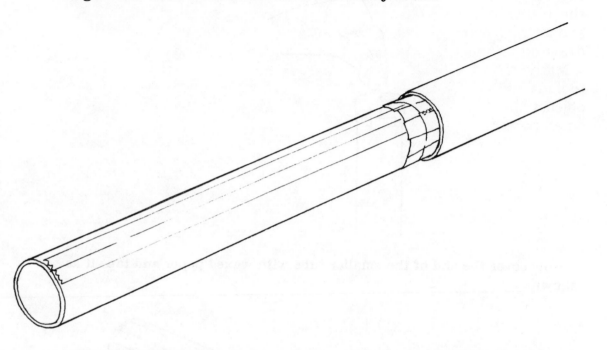

Look at an electric light with your camera obscura. Or, take it outside on a sunny day and look at a tree or a tall building. **(BE CAREFUL NOT TO LOOK AT THE SUN SINCE THIS COULD DAMAGE YOUR EYES.)**

If you move the smaller tube back and forth inside the larger one, you should be able to bring different objects into focus on the piece of waxed paper. The objects will always appear upside-down, since the same principle is working in the camera obscura you have made as in the one described by Alhazen 1,000 years ago.

Even though Alhazen's book on optics was known in Europe during the 1200s, little attention was paid to the camera obscura until the 1400s. An important change took place at that time. European artists had become more interested in the problem of accurately drawing animals, people, landscapes and buildings.

Many of these Renaissance artists used the camera obscura as a tool. It helped them accurately copy the lines and shapes of the objects they were drawing. Their camera obscuras were actually small portable rooms that they carried around with them. The artist would get inside the room and trace the landscapes or buildings on a piece of transparent paper that was placed over a glass viewing screen.

An engraving of a large camera obscura from the 1600s. The top and front are cut away to show an artist tracing, from behind, the images cast by the lens onto a piece of transparent paper. *Courtesy George Eastman House, Rochester*

## CONVEX LENS

**An oval lens which has a surface that curves or bulges outward so that it is thicker in the middle than at the ends.**

## FOCAL POINT

**The point in back of the lens at which the rays of light meet and form a clear image.**

An important improvement was made on the camera obscura in the mid-1500s. A **convex lens** was placed in the opening in the side of the camera box. By using a convex lens, the **focal point** was shortened. The image was also made much clearer. This happened because the convex lens bent the light inward.

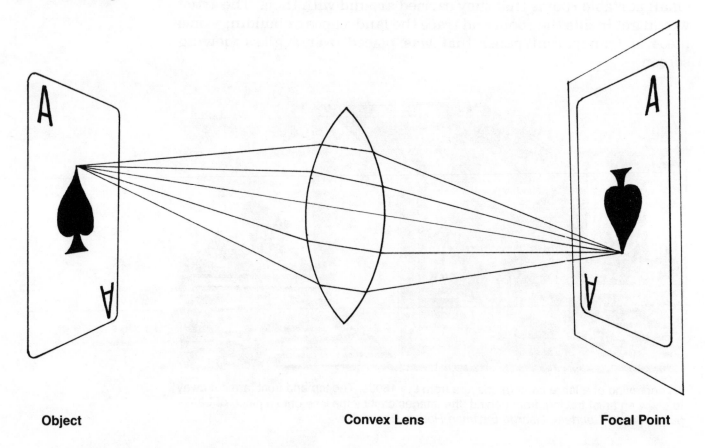

**Object**                    **Convex Lens**                    **Focal Point**

An illustration of an artist's portable camera obscura from the 1800s shows the convex lens inserted into the side of the camera box. The image was formed by the lens and reflected by the mirror onto the piece of glass. The artist then traced the reflection seen on the piece of glass. The compactness of this camera obscura simplified its use by artists not only in their studios, but also outdoors. Notice that the artist is using the top cover to shield the drawing area from outside light so that he can see the image more clearly.

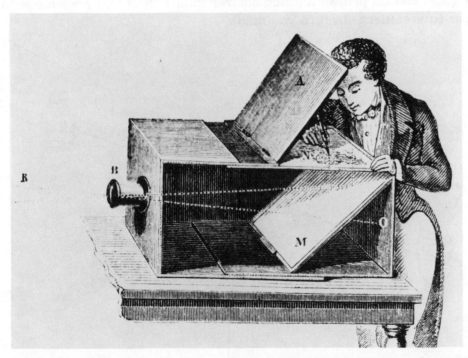

A portable artist's camera obscura from the early 1800s. *Courtesy George Eastman House, Rochester*

You can best understand how a convex lens works by using one to focus the image of a bright object, such as a light bulb, onto a piece of blank white paper. A magnifying glass will work very well as your convex lens.

Hold the magnifying glass steady a couple of feet away from the source of light. Move the sheet of paper back and forth until the image of the light bulb, which will be inverted, comes into focus on the paper. The magnifying glass should project a much clearer image than was possible with the paper-tube camera obscura you made.

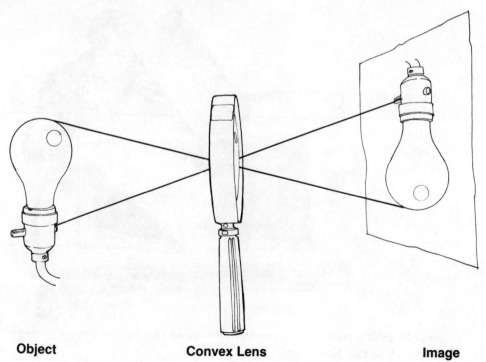

**Object**                    **Convex Lens**                    **Image**

The camera obscura, whether it uses a lens or a small hole to focus the image, contains all of the basic parts of a modern photographic camera. In fact, you can build a slightly more complicated camera obscura to view images and even take photographs!

In order to make this type of camera obscura or **pinhole camera**, you will need the following materials:

A 20″ x 30″ sheet of ¹⁄₁₆″-thick cardboard

Black masking tape (You can use black plastic electrician's tape as a substitute.)

Number 10 needle

X-Acto knife

Scissors

Ruler

Straightedge (to use when cutting edges)

White glue

1″ square of aluminum foil

Flat black spray paint

Large sheet of waxed paper

Old newspaper

Optional:

A 1″ square of brass shim stock (Available at an auto-supply or hardware store. Aluminum flashing can also be used.)

Very fine emery paper

Copy the patterns for the camera obscura included between pages 42 and 43 by tracing them onto pieces of white paper or by duplicating them. Cut out the patterns and tape them onto the cardboard.

## PINHOLE CAMERA

The basic principles of a pinhole camera were first published in the book, *Magias Naturalis* (The Secrets of Natural Magic), in 1558. The book was written by an alchemist—Giovanni della Porta, of Naples, Italy. In the revised 1589 edition, della Porta included a description of a camera obscura with a lens instead of the pinhole to focus the image.

In order to maintain light-safe conditions, the inside of the finished camera and all accessories must be painted flat black. You will find it easier to mark and spray all of the pieces before you assemble them. Use a fast-drying spray paint. Place the pieces on old newspapers while spraying to prevent overspray.

Use the X-Acto knife and a straightedge to cut out the right side, left side, top and bottom of the camera.

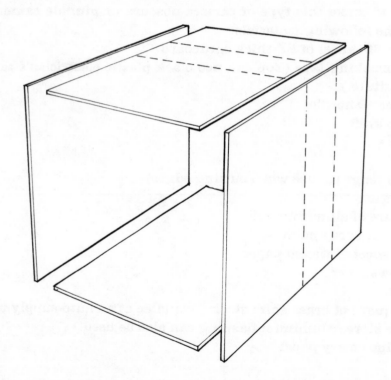

Tape the piece of waxed paper to the top of your worktable. It will protect the table and keep the camera from sticking to the surface of the table while you are building it.

Apply a thin bead of glue along one of the 5″ edges of the bottom piece of the camera.

Place the bottom piece of the camera flat on the waxed paper. Slide one 5″ x 5″ side against the glued edge of the bottom piece.

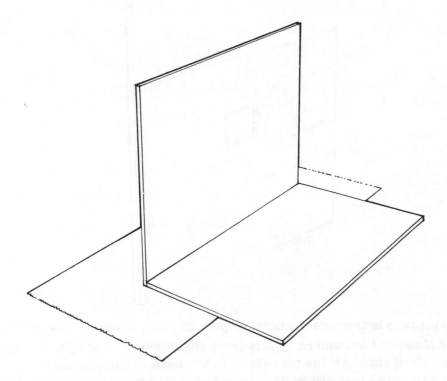

Repeat the same gluing steps for the other 5″ x 5″ side of the camera.

Turn the unit upside-down and glue the top piece in place just as you glued the sides and bottom together. You should now have a 4″ x 5″ box unit.

Cut out the front piece of the camera. Next, cut out the ⅜" square hole in the front piece of the camera.

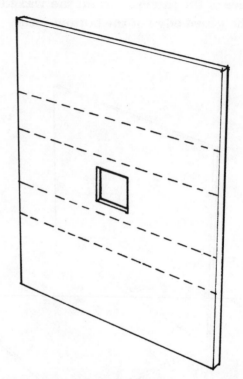

The pinhole is the most important part of your camera because it works as the lens for the camera. Light from the object you are photographing focuses itself through the pinhole onto the back of the camera.

You can make two different types of pinholes for your camera. For the first, a number 10 needle is used to punch the pinhole into a piece of aluminum foil. In the second, a piece of very thin brass shim stock or aluminum flashing is used. The hole is also drilled with a number 10 needle. Sand lightly around the hole with the emery paper to make it a smooth opening.

Both of these methods will work, but the pinhole drilled into the piece of brass is much more accurate and will produce a much better image and picture.

Decide whether you are going to use a piece of aluminum foil, brass shim stock or aluminum flashing for your pinhole plate. Punch the hole in the exact center of the plate.

Tape the pinhole plate to the inside of the front piece of the camera so that the pinhole is exactly in the center of the ⅜″ square.

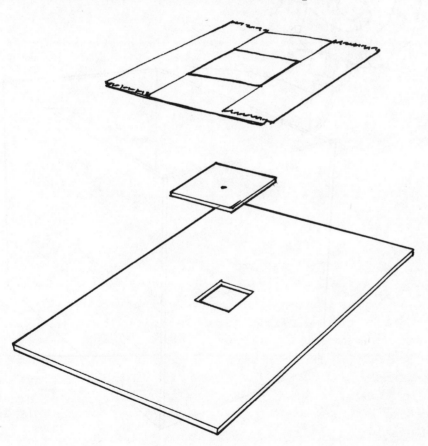

Apply a bead of glue all around the front side of the camera box. Then glue the front panel in place.

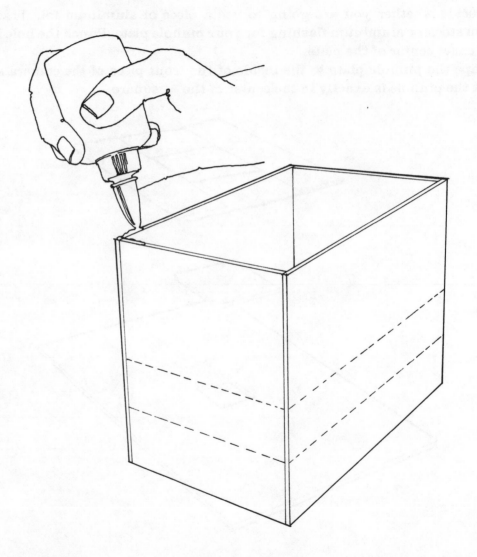

**Set the camera box unit aside to dry.**

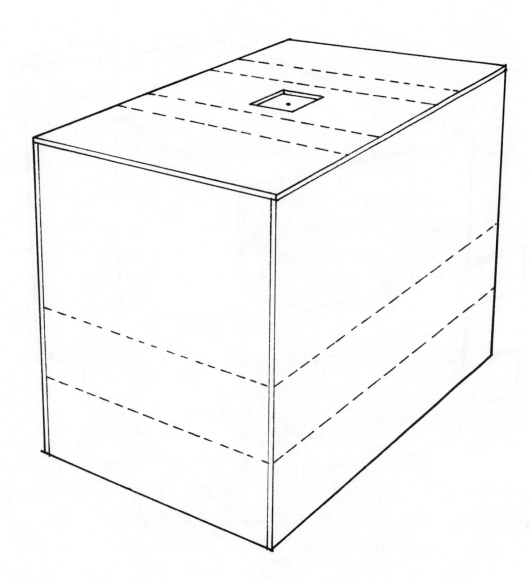

Cut out the shutter-bracket steps. Glue them into position on the front panel of the camera box as shown.

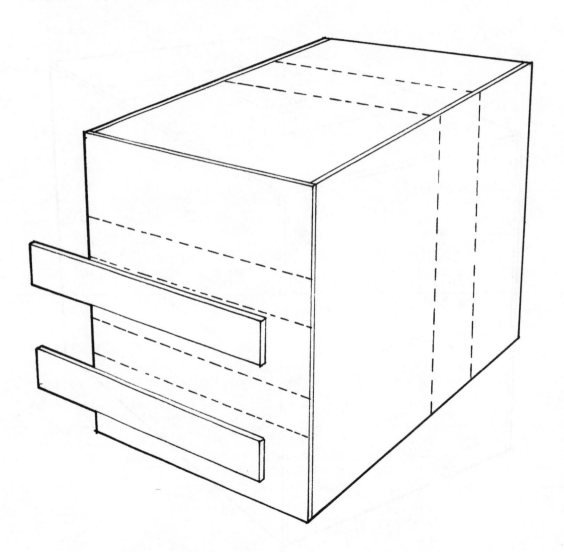

Cut out the shutter-brackets and glue them to the bracket steps as illustrated.

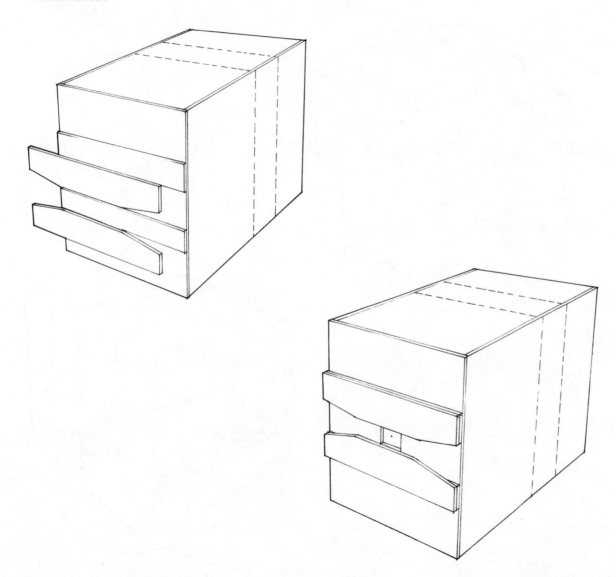

Cut out the 4″ x 1″ patterns for the accessory stops. Glue them around the end of the camera body as shown.

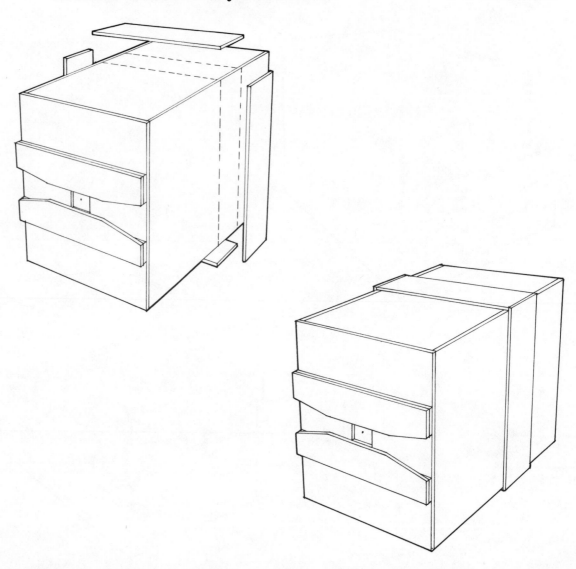

Cut out two pieces of cardboard 4$\frac{1}{16}$″ x 18″. Cut out two more pieces, 5$\frac{3}{16}$″ x 18″.

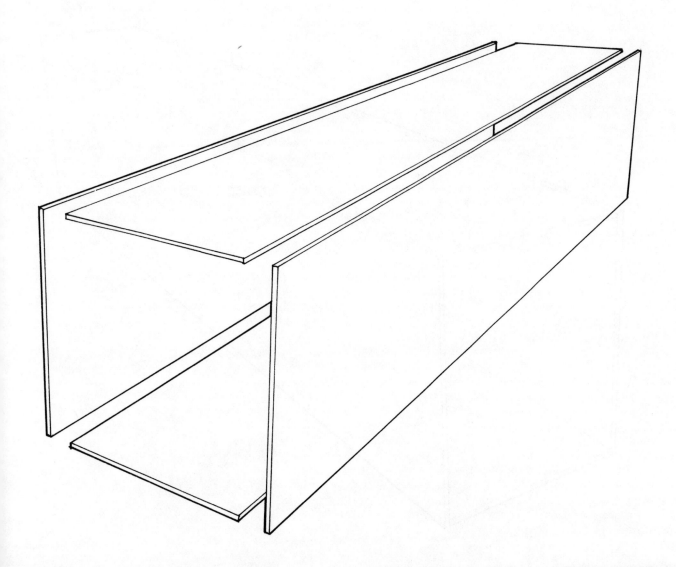

Glue these pieces together in the same way you assembled the camera body.

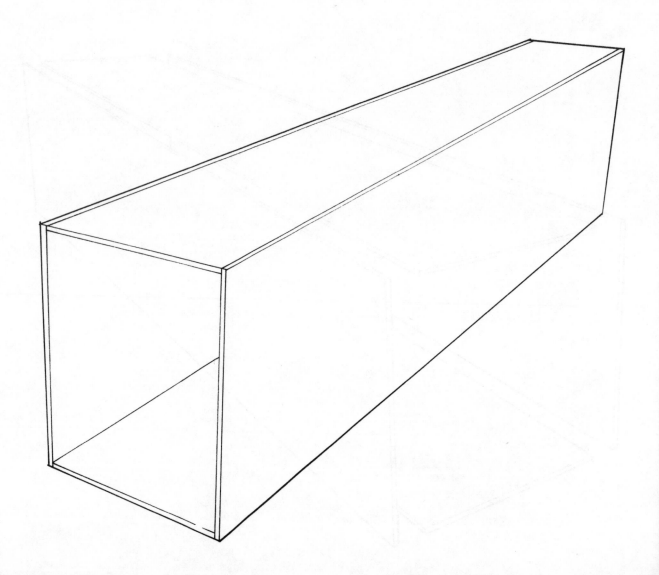

Reinforce all outer joints of the camera and the tube with ¾" black masking tape as shown.

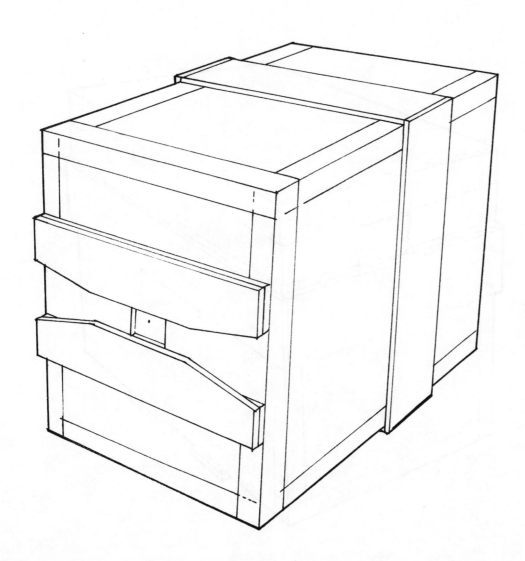

Before you begin to experiment with taking your own pictures, you can see how your camera obscura works. Tape a piece of waxed paper over the back of the camera.

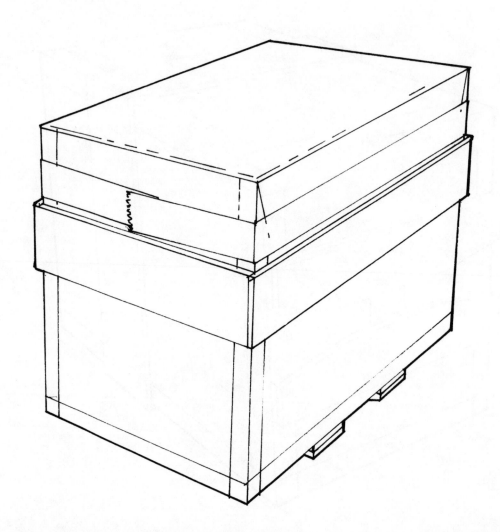

**Place the tube over the waxed paper as illustrated.**

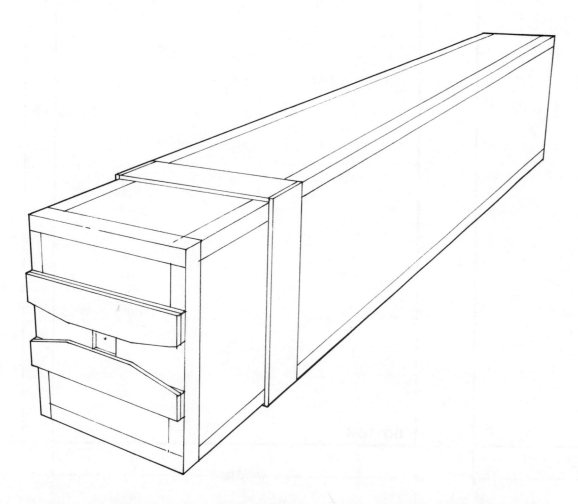

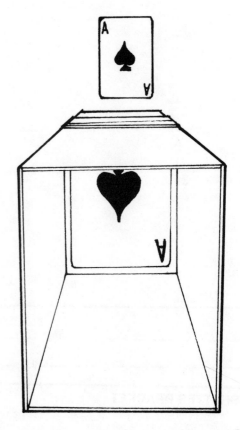

Now aim the camera at a bright object either indoors or outdoors. Look through the tube. You should be able to see an inverted image of the object you are looking at.

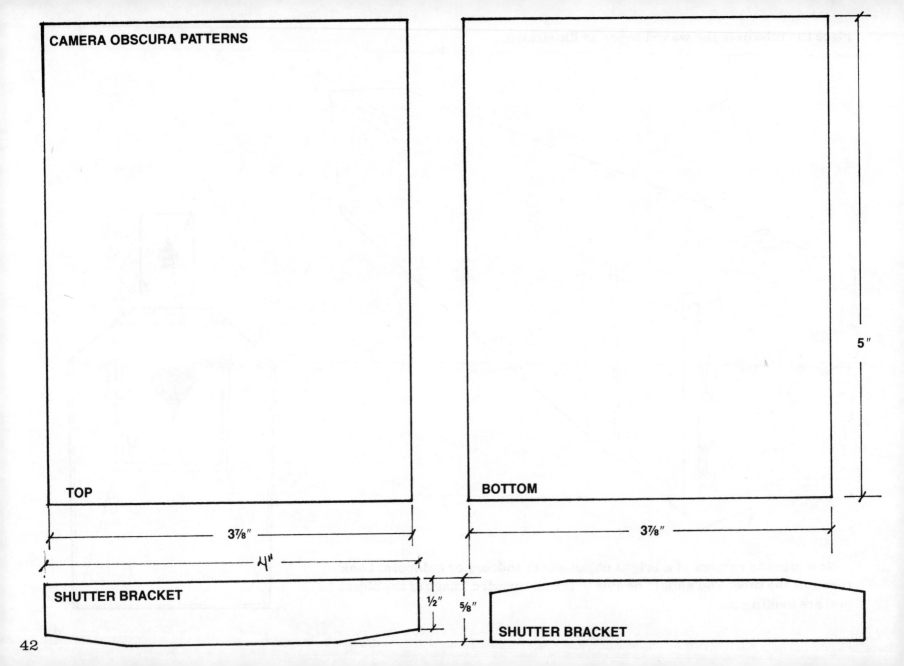

**CAMERA OBSCURA PATTERNS**

TOP

BOTTOM

5"

3⅞"

3⅞"

4"

SHUTTER BRACKET

½"

5⁄8"

SHUTTER BRACKET

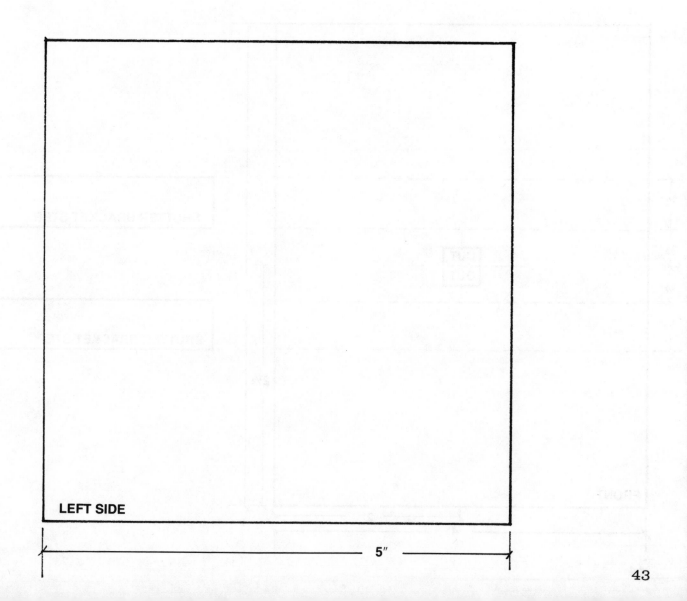

**LEFT SIDE**

5″

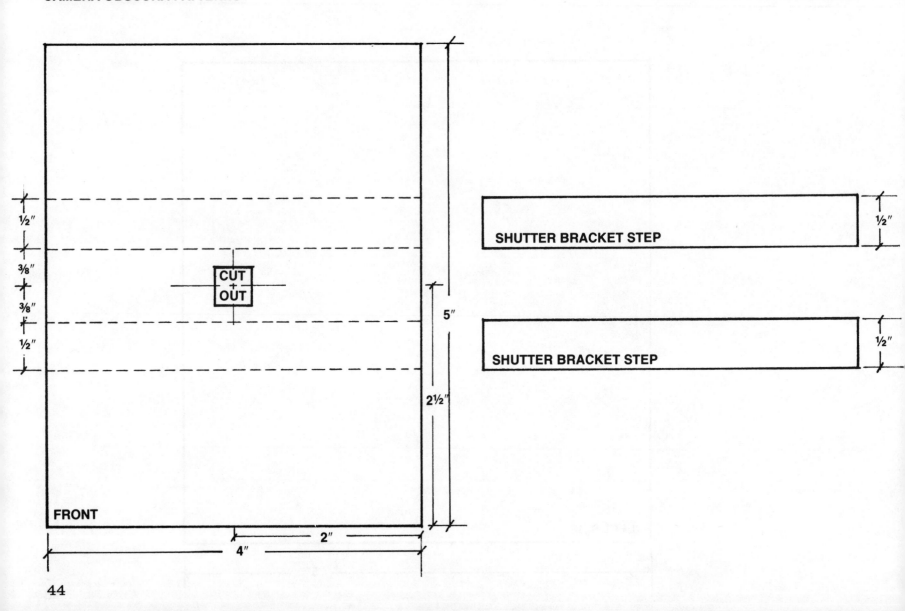

## CAMERA OBSCURA PATTERNS

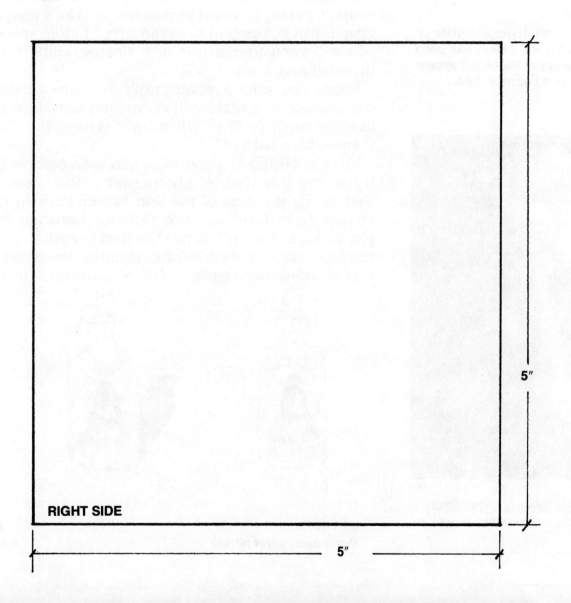

**RIGHT SIDE**

5"

5"

## NEGATIVE

**The exposed film or photographic plate on which the image of a real object has been developed. Light areas of the object appear dark and the dark areas appear light.**

Johann Heinrich Schulze (1687-1744)
*Courtesy George Eastman House, Rochester*

If you were to remove the waxed paper and put the back panel of the camera in its place with a piece of unexposed film or photographic paper, it would be possible to take a simple **negative** photograph. But before you take the first photograph with your camera, you will need to discover how photographic film and paper were invented and work.

When you take a photograph you are changing the chemical composition of a silver-salt compound imbedded in a piece of photographic paper or film. When light strikes the silver salts, it causes them to turn dark.

The darkening of silver salts had been observed by scientists long before the invention of photography. But these scientists believed that air or the heat of the sun rather than light, caused them to change from light to dark. Johann Heinrich Schulze, a German physician and scientist, was the first person to prove that light from the sun was responsible for darkening the silver salts. Schulze did this by covering a glass bottle containing a mixture of chalk and

**Unexposed silver nitrate**                    **Darkened silver nitrate**

46

**silver nitrate** with paper cut-outs in the shape of letters of the alphabet. Where the letters protected the mixture from the sun's rays, it remained light, while the remaining unprotected mixture of silver salts darkened.

Schulze did not try to make the images of the letters permanent. Even so, it was this **photochemical reaction** which he observed and wrote about that was to become the basis for modern photography.

About 1800, an Englishman, Thomas Wedgewood, tried to **fix** the image from a camera obscura. He was unable to produce clear images using the camera obscura. So, Wedgewood resorted to laying leaves and insect wings on paper and leather coated with light-sensitive silver nitrate. Then he exposed them to the sunlight.

Wedgewood was able to make a negative image in his experiment, since all of the parts of the paper or leather that were not covered turned black. Unfortunately, he could not find a way to fix his negative pictures and make them permanent. When they were further exposed to light, they would turn completely black.

**SILVER NITRATE**

**A poisonous, colorless crystalline compound, known as AgNO₃. It turns greyish-black when exposed to light and combined with organic matter.**

**PHOTOCHEMICAL REACTION**

**A reaction caused by the interaction of radiant energy or light and chemicals.**

**FIX**

**To prevent a change in shade or color of a photograph by washing or coating it with a chemical that preserves the image.**

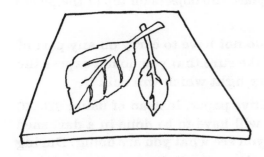

**Unexposed leather treated with silver nitrate.**

**Exposed leather treated with silver nitrate.**

A portrait of Thomas Wedgewood.

**SODIUM CHLORIDE (NaCl)**

A colorless crystalline compound which is used in the manufacture of seasonings. It is also known as common salt or table salt.

**SAFELIGHT**

A light bulb or lamp which has one or more color filters that allow just enough light for a darkroom without exposing photographic film or paper.

You can re-create the basic elements of Wedgewood's experiment using a few simple materials:

Two 5″ x 7″ photo trays filled with water
1 teaspoon **sodium chloride** (table salt)
1 teaspoon silver nitrate
5 or 6 plain index cards or 3″ x 5″ white cards
Tongs
Paper towels
Simple objects, such as coins, key, or buttons, that can be placed on top of the index cards

If it is inconvenient for you to make your own light-sensitive paper, you can buy a small package of STUDIO PROOF PAPER from a photography store to use to make your sunprints. Substitute the STUDIO PROOF PAPER for the light-sensitive paper you would have made yourself. Then jump ahead to the part of the experiment where you place the objects on top of the pieces of paper.

If you use STUDIO PROOF PAPER, you do not have to carry on any part of the experiment in a darkened room. Make sure that you do not expose the light-sensitive paper to any unnecessary light which will ruin it.

If you do make your own light-sensitive paper, instead of using STUDIO PROOF PAPER, part of this experiment will have to be done in a darkened room. You can use a **safelight** to help you see what you are doing. During the first part of the experiment you can leave the lights on.

Dissolve one teaspoon sodium chloride in the water in one of the photo trays. Then dissolve one teaspoon silver nitrate in the other tray full of water. BE VERY CAREFUL NOT TO GET ANY OF THE SILVER NITRATE ON YOUR HANDS SINCE IT WILL STAIN YOUR SKIN DARK BROWN AND IS VERY DIFFICULT TO WASH OFF.

Pick up a couple of the index cards with the tongs and soak the cards in the sodium-chloride solution. Remove the index cards from the sodium-chloride solution. Let them drain on a paper towel.

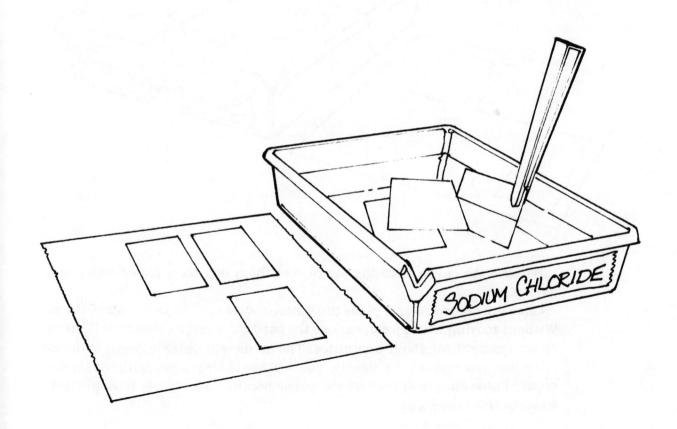

Now turn off the lights. If you have a safelight, you can leave it on. Pick up the index cards (which should still be slightly wet) with the tongs and place them in the pan with the dissolved silver nitrate for 3 to 5 minutes.

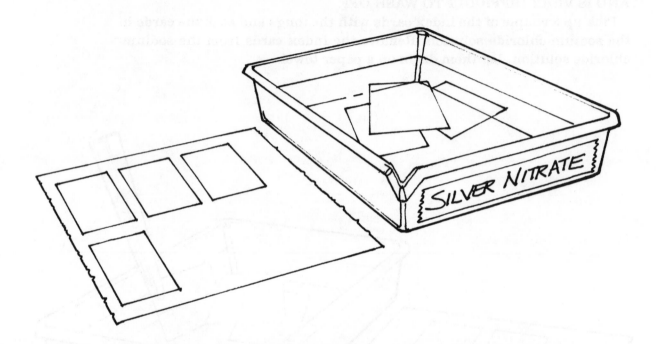

Remove the cards with the tongs. Let them dry on a paper towel in a dark place.

Once the cards are dry, place the buttons, coins, or keys on top of them. Without moving the objects, expose the cards to a bright electrical light or direct sunlight for about 5 minutes. The cards will quickly begin to darken. When you remove the objects, you will see their shapes outlined on the paper. These shapes appear on the paper because the objects have protected them from the light.

You have discovered in your experiment exactly what Thomas Wedgewood did when he created his sunprints. The sodium chloride was combined with the silver nitrate on the paper card. A chemical reaction took place and a new compound was created which is called silver chloride (AgCl). When the light struck the specially prepared paper, the energy in the light separated the silver from the silver chloride. This caused the exposed paper to darken. The equation for this chemical reaction is:

$$NaCl + AgNO_3 \xrightarrow{\text{sunlight}} NaNO_3 + AgCl$$

Your images will also fade very quickly once they are exposed to the light, and will soon turn completely black. In order to prevent the images from fading, a method of fixing the image or making it permanent had to be invented.

The Frenchman, Joseph Nicephore Niepce, was the first person to permanently fix the image from a camera obscura. In 1816, Niepce took a series of pictures on paper treated with silver chloride. However, he was unable to remove the unexposed silver salts from the paper in order to obtain a permanent image.

Niepce continued experimenting with light-sensitive substances. Finally, he tried bitumen of Judea, a type of asphalt, which hardened instead of changing color when it was exposed to light. It is believed that he was able to take the world's first successful photograph in 1822, using bitumen of Judea as a fixer. Niepce's first photographs had to be exposed to sunlight for as long as eight hours!

In 1829, Niepce, who was in ill health and running out of money, formed a partnership with Louis Jacques Mande Daguerre. Daguerre was a famous inventor and painter of huge diorama scenes.

The diorama was an actual theater in which large pieces of cloth, sometimes as big as 45 x 70 feet, were painted on both sides with dramatic scenes. When the lighting was moved from the top of the painting to the back, it appeared to the audience that one scene dissolved into another.

Joseph Niepce (1765-1833)

Earliest known photograph of the view of a building, seen from his room, taken by Niepce in 1826. *Courtesy The Gernsheim Collection, University of Texas*

Daguerre's Diorama

Daguerre (1787–1851)

Daguerre often used the camera obscura to make the paintings for his diorama. So he was very interested in finding a way to permanently fix the images which were reflected at the back of the camera. If he could do this, he would be able to copy them exactly.

After Niepce's death in 1833, Daguerre tried to perfect his own method of photography. At first he experimented with bichloride of mercury, which barely brought out the images in his pictures.

It is said that one day Daguerre left an exposed plate in a cabinet in which a thermometer had broken. The mercury vapors from the broken thermometer actually developed his first photographic image. It was not until 1837 that Daguerre succeeded in fixing and making his image permanent. He used a salt solution and hot water to dissolve away the particles of silver iodine not affected by the light. He made this invention known to the world in 1839.

The basic steps in Daguerre's method for taking a photographic image were:

1. A plate of copper was covered with a thin sheet of silver.

2. Small balls of cotton were used to rub pumice powder and oil into the silver.

3. The plate was then buffed with a piece of padded buckskin mounted on a flat wooden board.

Polishing the daguerreotype plate with pumice.

Buffing the daguerreotype plate.

**IODINE**

A mineral, in the form of dark crystals that is used as a chemical element.

**BROMINE**

A reddish-brown liquid that gives off a strong vapor.

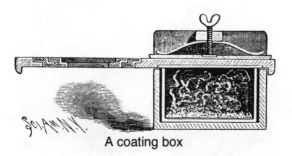

A coating box

4. The dulled silver plate was then coated with **iodine** by exposing it to fumes of iodine which made it sensitive to light. The same coating process was repeated, using **bromine.**

5. In a darkroom, the prepared plate was checked for scratches or flaws in front of a filtered yellow light. It was then placed on a small board and slipped in a camera.

Checking the daguerreotype plate for flaws.

6. The camera was then put on a tripod and pointed at an object or subject in the direct sunlight.

7. When the lens of the camera was uncovered, the plate was exposed to the light for about 15 to 30 minutes.

Exposing a daguerreotype plate in a studio.

8. The latent, or hidden image, was then developed and made permanent.

Daguerre's developing-and-fixing process involved the following steps.

1. The plate was placed in a cabinet at a 45-degree angle above a pan holding two pounds of mercury. The spirit lamp, which heated the mercury to 150° F., was placed under this pan.

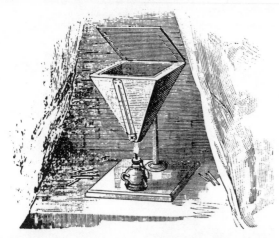

Developing a daguerreotype plate with a spirit lamp, which uses alcohol or some other type of liquid fuel.

2. The plate was carefully watched through a glass spy hole until the image became visible. This happened because the particles of mercury were adhering to the exposed silver.

3. Then the plate was plunged in cold water to harden its surface.

4. Next, the plate was submerged in a solution of common salt. Daguerre substituted hyposulphite of soda for the salt in this step of the process in 1839.

5. Finally, the plate was washed to stop the action of the salt as a fixing agent.

Using this process, Daguerre obtained a positive image which was reversed from what it was in real life. The image could only be seen when held at a certain angle in an indirect light. For example, if it was placed in direct sunlight, the picture appeared to only be a shiny sheet of silver. Daguerre's plate could not be multiplied or reproduced. Photographs made by Daguerre's process became known as **daguerreotypes.**

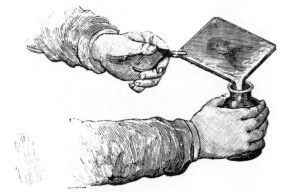

Washing the daguerreotype plate to stop the fixer.

Daguerreotypes opened up a whole new world. For the first time, almost anyone could have an exact image of themselves, or of their home, very inexpensively. And the image was permanent and could be passed on to their family after they were gone.

**DAGUERREOTYPE**
**The first successful photographic process and picture. An image was formed on a copper plate coated with polished silver by using vapors from heated mercury.**

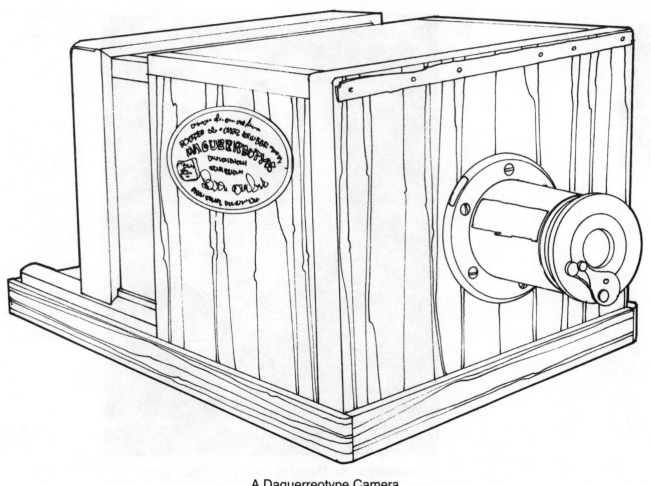

A Daguerreotype Camera

In standard sizes, matted, and framed in brass in a case, Daguerreotypes could be purchased in the early 1840s for two dollars. Since they required headrests to keep their subjects from moving during the long exposures, daguerreotype portraits usually appeared very formal and the people in them rarely smiled.

Daguerreotype by Daguerre of an unknown artist.
*Courtesy George Eastman House, Rochester*

Among the most famous early American daguerreotypists was Samuel F. B. Morse, a famous portrait painter and the inventor of the telegraph and Morse code. His student, Mathew B. Brady, was the most famous photographer of the Civil War.

Alexander Hesler. Daguerreotype of Ida Hesler, about 1854.
*Courtesy George Eastman House, Rochester*

Daguerreotype Headrest

## CAMERA LUCIDA

**An optical device that projects the image of an object onto a plane surface where it can be traced. It was invented in 1807 by William H. Wollaston to help artists draw objects, people and landscapes in the correct perspective.**

While Daguerre was perfecting his photographic process, the Englishman, W. H. Fox Talbot, was also making several extremely important discoveries. While on his honeymoon in Italy, Talbot had become interested in recording scenes from his trip. As he traveled, he used devices such as the camera obscura and the **camera lucida** to help him make drawings of different scenes he admired.

Talbot felt that his drawings were not good enough because he was not trained as an artist. It occurred to him, he wrote some years later, "how charming it would be if it were possible to cause these natural images to imprint themselves durably, and remain fixed upon the paper."

When he returned to England in 1834, Talbot began to experiment with sensitizing paper using solutions of table salt and silver nitrate. In doing so, he was testing through experimentation the theories he had developed while traveling in Italy.

As early as 1835, Talbot had experimented with placing pieces of light-sensitive paper in different types of very small cameras. His wife called these cameras mousetraps. Talbot tried to shorten the exposure time required to take a picture by inserting lenses into the mousetraps, which would focus the light on a smaller area. He used microscope lenses that made it possible to record a brighter image much faster.

The problem with the mousetraps was that the pictures were so small, only about one square inch. Talbot decided to quit working with them and concentrate his experiments on developing negative-photographic prints in the larger cameras being used at that time.

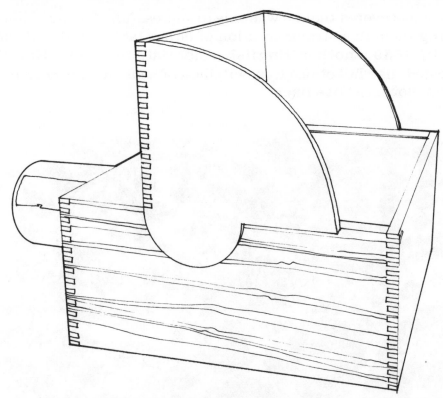

Fox Talbot's Camera Obscura

A carte-de-visite portrait of William Henry Fox Talbot by J. Moffat, Edinburgh. *Courtesy of History of Photography Collection, the Smithsonian Institution*

Talbot's method of making photographic negatives involved mixing different quantities of salt and silver nitrate, which combined together to form silver chloride. After repeating his experiments many times, Talbot discovered that the best results were produced by a very weak solution of salt combined with silver nitrate on the paper's surface. He then placed flat objects, such as leaves and lace, on paper treated with salt and silver nitrate. When exposed to the sunlight, negative images appeared on the paper.

Talbot discovered that he was able to successfully fix his images by washing them in a strong solution of either table salt or potassium salt. In 1839 another English scientist, Sir John Herschel, suggested that Talbot use hyposulphate of soda, which proved to be an even more effective fixer.

Lace. A. "photogenic drawing" from the *Pencil of Nature*, by Fox Talbot. It was the first book to use photographs as illustrations and was published between 1844 and 1846. *Courtesy of the Library of Congress*

You can re-create Talbot's method for fixing and making permanent negative pictures by using the following materials:

   Piece of unexposed, light-sensitive paper from the earlier Wedgewood experiment
   5″ x 7″ photo tray filled with cold water
   ¼ cup table salt (NaCl)
   Paper towel

Stir the table salt into the water until it is completely dissolved.

As in the Wedgewood experiment, place various objects on top of the specially treated, light-sensitive paper. Then expose the paper to a bright light or direct sunlight.

Once the outlines of the objects appear on the paper, wash it thoroughly in the water-and-salt solution.

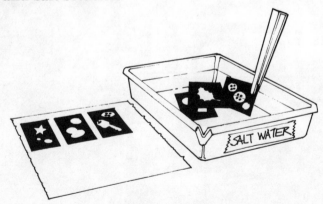

When you have finished washing the paper, place it on a paper towel to dry. The outlines of the objects should remain permanent, no matter how much the paper is exposed to light.

In 1840, Talbot announced that he had successfully captured permanent images on paper. The fuzzy, softly defined image on a paper negative became known as a "calotype." The advantage of the calotype was that an unlimited number of prints could be made from the paper negative. The method is therefore considered to be the basis for the negative-positive photographic process used all over the world today.

Calotype of Frederick's Photographic Temple of Art, New York City, circa 1850. *Courtesy of the National Archives.*

In a negative print, shaded areas are light and light areas are shaded. In order to obtain a positive print, which represents what the object photographed actually looks like, the process must be reversed. Talbot produced positive prints by projecting light through his paper negatives onto the same specially treated paper with which he made his original negative. By inventing this process, he was able to create the first real positive-photographic print.

**Paper negative**

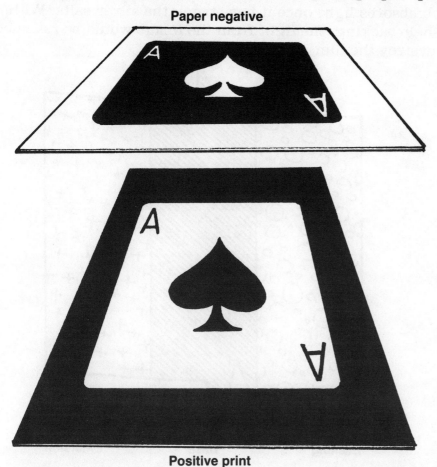

**Positive print**

## EMULSION

A light-sensitive coating on photographic plates, paper and film that reacts with light to form a latent or hidden image.

## SILVER BROMIDE (AgBr)

A pale-yellow crystalline compound which turns black when exposed to light. It is used as a light-sensitive element on photographic paper, glass and film.

## GELATIN BASE

A colorless or slightly yellow, transparent protein which is made by boiling prepared skins, bones and connective tissues of animals. It is used in foods, drugs and photographic film.

It is easy to see the similarity between Talbot's paper negatives and plastic-photographic negatives. Modern photographic film consists of a sheet of clear plastic with a thin coating called an **emulsion.** The emulsion is made up of tiny grains of silver salts, **silver bromide** and silver iodine. These are adhered to the palstic by a **gelatin base.** On the other side of the piece of plastic, opposite the silver salts and gelatin base, is an anti-halo backing. This is a dye which absorbs light once it has struck the silver salts. Without the anti-halo backing, the light from the image would be reflected back and destroy the film.

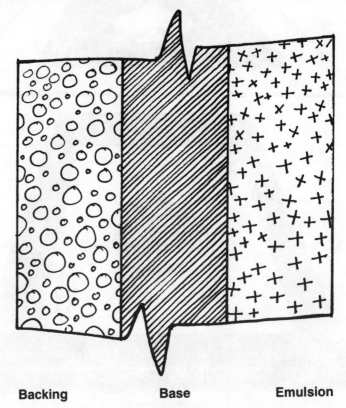

**Backing**  **Base**  **Emulsion**

A different method than Talbot's was invented in 1847 by Felix Abel Niepce de St. Victor (a cousin of Nicephore Niepce). He had experimented with various methods of adhering light-sensitive silver salts to a piece of clear glass. Earlier experiments had included the use of adhesive materials as unusual as the slime secreted by snails. Finally, St. Victor's experiments were successful using a backing made from egg whites. But Niepce de St. Victor's photographs, which were known as **albumen** prints, did not become particularly popular with photographers since they required very long exposures.

**ALBUMEN**
**A nutritive substance, such as the white of an egg, which surrounds a developing embryo.**

Advertisement from the 1860s. *Courtesy George Eastman House, Rochester*

## GUNCOTTON
**An explosive made of cellulose treated with sulfuric and nitric acids.**

## ETHER ($C_4H_{10}O$)
**A highly flammable liquid that is made from distilled ethyl alcohol and sulfuric acid.**

A buffer used to polish collodion plates.

In 1851, a new process was developed by English sculptor Frederick Scott Archer. It was to have a great impact on the history of photography. Archer's method mixed **guncotton** with **ether** to make a solution which he called "collodion." This was a word he made up based upon the Greek word *kolla*, which means "glue." Archer's collodion method was a great improvement. It made it possible to make a negative image on a glass plate for reproduction of an unlimited number of very high-quality positive prints. Since the negatives could not be enlarged though, the camera had to be as big as the desired print!

In the first step of the collodion method, the glass plate would be polished with a buffer. Next, the collodion mixture was prepared. Potassium iodide was mixed into it and the resulting compound was then spread over a piece of glass.

Coating the collodion plate.

Once the mixture was spread over the glass, it was dipped in silver nitrate and exposed in a camera while it was still wet. It is because of this step that the collodion method became known as the "wet-plate" process.

The glass plate was developed. Then the collodion image could be peeled away from the glass plate to which it had been adhered. Next, the image was fixed.

The wet-plate process produced negatives that could be viewed as positives by simply placing them against a dark cloth background or by painting the back of the negative black. Extremely inexpensive photographs, known as "ambrotypes," could be produced using this method.

Ambrotypes were very popular throughout the United States during the late 1850s. Like daguerreotypes, they came in standard sizes and were often matted, then framed in elaborate gilded-brass frames that came in protective cases.

An interesting variation of the collodion wet-plate method of photography was the extremely popular tintype or ferrotype. In this process the positive photograph was made directly on a brown- or black-enameled tinplate sheet instead of on a glass plate.

Immersing the collodion plate.

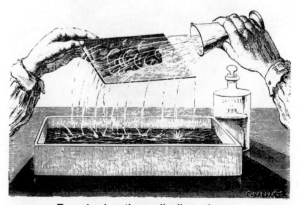

Developing the collodion plate.

Not only were tintypes easy and cheap to make, but they were stronger than glass plates and could easily be exchanged through the mail with little fear of damage. During the late 1800s, hundreds of thousands of Americans had their tintype portraits made in studios like the one set up in 1890 by Frances B. Johnston.

Tintype from the 1870s.

An ambrotype with the black backing on one half to show how a negative image is turned into a positive one. *Courtesy George Eastman House, Rochester*

Frances B. Johnston. Tintype Studio, about 1890. *Courtesy George Eastman House, Rochester*

Johnston began her career as a photographer in 1888. At first she was famous for her portraits, including those of several United States presidents. By the turn of the century she had also become famous as a press photographer who recorded major news events all over the world. In fact, Johnston took the last photograph of President William McKinley just before he was assassinated at the Pan American Exposition in 1901. In her later years, Johnston used photography to record and document many of the beautiful gardens, old homes and buildings in the Southeastern United States.

Even more popular than the tintype during the mid- and late-1800s was the inexpensive carte de visite process. It was patented in 1854 by Frenchman André Adolphe E. Disdéri. Carte de visite is the name given to both Disdéri's special camera and the photographs it produced. The camera had four or more lenses which could take multiple images on a single wet-plate negative.

The positive print from the one large negative was cut up into individual photographs. These usually measured about 3½" x 2⅛". They were attached to cards the size of visiting or calling cards. Since these inexpensive portraits were often left by visitors in place of printed calling cards, they became known as cartes de visites.

In both Europe and the United States, cartes de visites greatly changed photography. They were exchanged on birthdays and holidays. People everywhere began to assemble special albums full of the cards. They also collected images of famous people such as Queen Victoria, President Lincoln, and General Grant and his family.

During the 1800s, some important innovations were made in photography because of discoveries made in physics. One of the most important of these discoveries for photography was the stereoscope. By the 1840s, the first stereoscopic photographs had been taken. During the 1850s, cameras using a special system of lenses had been invented that allowed two slightly different pictures to be taken of the same object at once. Each lens was 2½ inches from the other so that the two different pictures recorded were exactly what would be seen by each of your eyes. When the developed stereographic print was placed in a stereoscope, a three-dimensional picture was created.

A carte de visite from the 1880s.

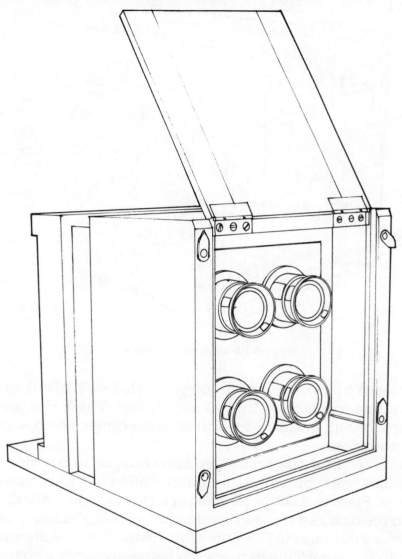

A carte de visite camera with four lenses.

LIEUT. GEN. GRANT

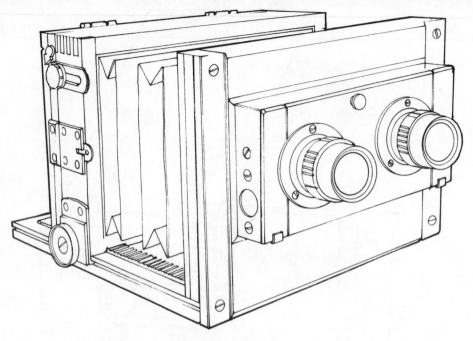

A Stereoscopic Camera.

It had been known for over 2,000 years that each of our eyes sees a different image when we look at something. These two images are combined in our brain to give us a three-dimensional view of the world around us.

You can see how the brain combines images into a single three-dimensional view by using the simple diagram illustrated on the next page. Place a small paper card at a right angle to the dotted line between the bird and the cage as the man is doing in the illustration. Now lower your nose to the edge of the card. The bird should appear to fly into the cage! This happened because your brain combined the two different images together to make a complete picture, which is three-dimensional.

A bust as viewed by each of the two eyes separately.

In 1832, the English physicist, Sir Charles Wheatstone, discovered how to make stereoscopic pictures. He prepared two drawings of the same object from slightly different viewpoints as seen by each of his eyes. These two drawings could be combined into a three-dimensional picture when viewed through a special mirrored device.

Wheatstone's device was called a stereoscope. Two mirrors were set so that their backs formed an angle of 90 degrees with each other. These mirrors were attached to a board. At the ends of the board were two panels where two slightly different drawings were placed. When the stereoscope was brought close to the face, each eye saw the image reflected from the two ends of the instrument in a different mirror. The mirrors combined the images to form a three-dimensional picture.

Wheatstone's Stereoscope

You can make a stereoscope just like Wheatstone's with the following materials:

2 small rectangular pocket mirrors
Piece of medium-weight cardboard
X-Acto knife or scissors
White glue
Tracing paper or thin white paper

Copy the patterns between pages 82 to 85 on the tracing paper. Mount them on the cardboard and cut out the pieces.

Glue the mirrors on the spaces marked with dotted lines and assemble the main part of your reflecting stereoscope as illustrated below.

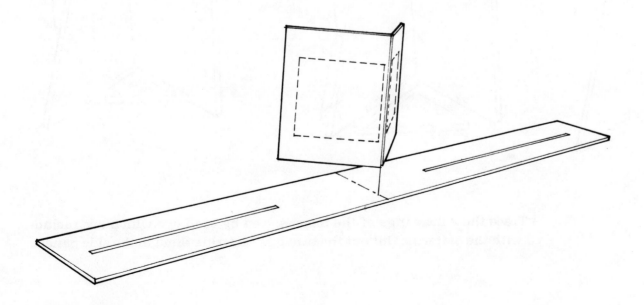

**Assemble the side panels of the stereoscope as shown below.**

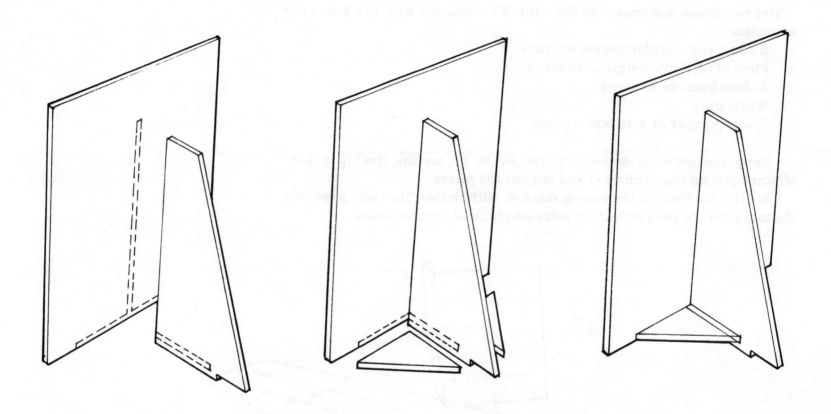

Trace the 2 drawings of the images seen by each eye which are included with the patterns. Cut out the tracings and glue them to the side panels.

Mount the side panels onto the main body of the stereoscope as illustrated.

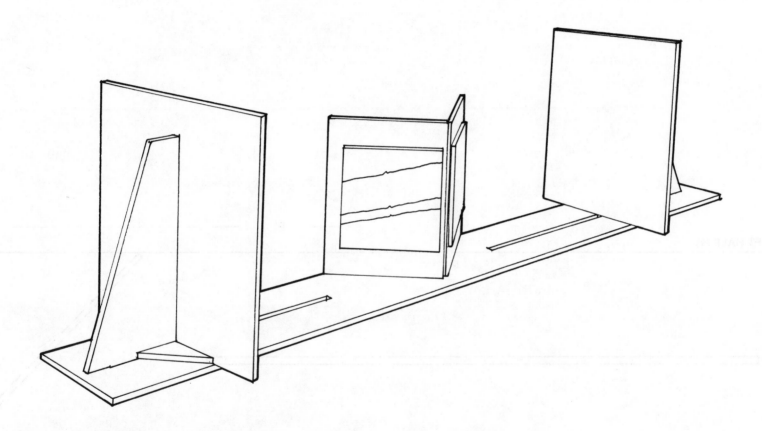

When you bring your assembled stereoscope close to your face, your eyes will see the separate images reflected in the 2 mirrors where they will form a combined three-dimensional picture.

# STEREOSCOPE PATTERNS

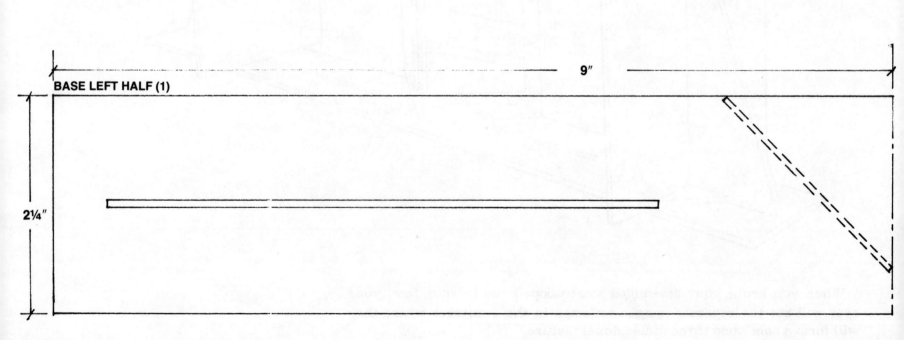

**BASE LEFT HALF (1)**

2¼"

9"

**BASE RIGHT HALF (1)**

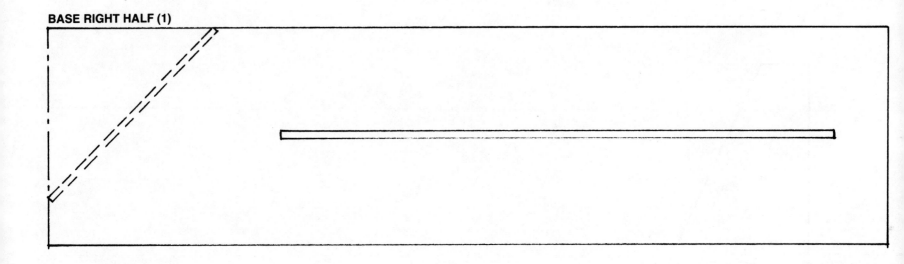

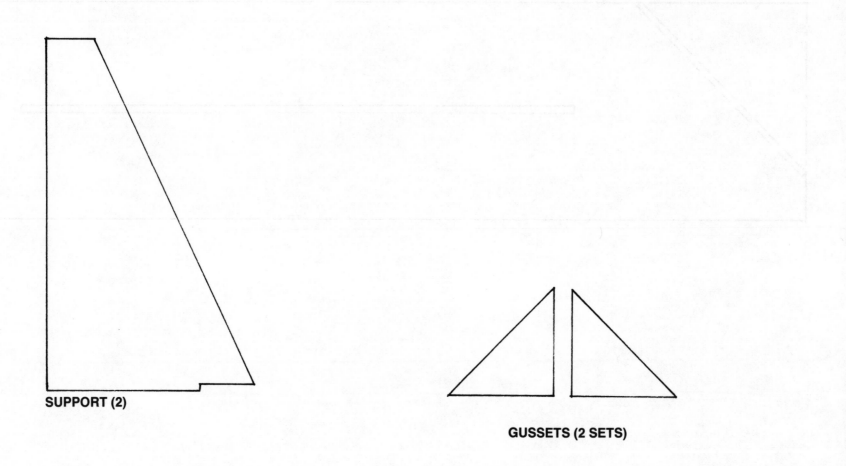

**SUPPORT (2)**

**GUSSETS (2 SETS)**

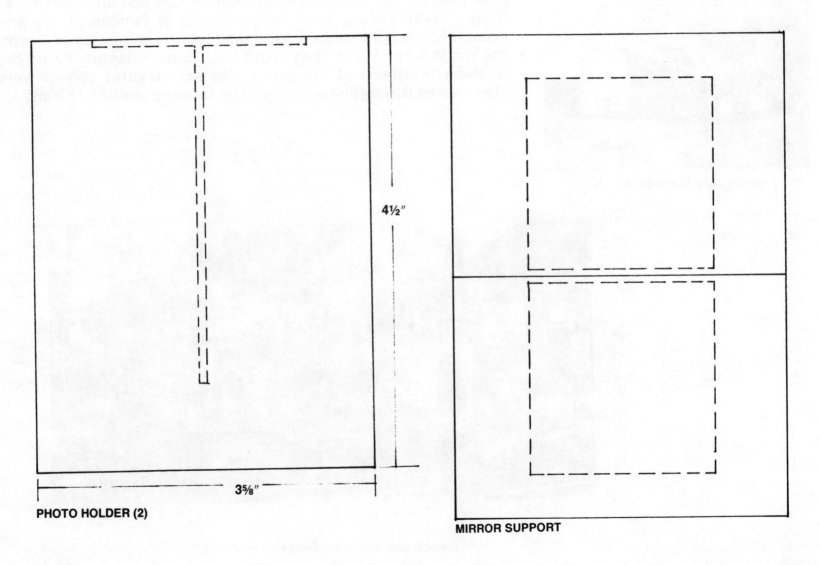

**4½"**

**3⅝"**

**PHOTO HOLDER (2)**

**MIRROR SUPPORT**

A stereoscope from the early 1800s.

Wheatstone's discovery of stereo effects was quickly applied to photography. Photographers throughout Europe and the United States began taking stereoscopic views of famous places and events. Stereoscopic cards were made of the pyramids of Egypt, the World's Fairs, the Holy Land and China. Niagara Falls, the Western frontier and humorous and sentimental scenes were also viewed through stereoscopes by thousands of Americans.

Stereoscope card of the Paris Exhibition, 1857.

It became very popular to collect stereoscopic cards during the mid-1800s. No matter where you lived in the United States, you could sit at home with your viewer and card collection and enjoy humorous and entertaining three-dimensional views of fantastic, faraway places.

Stereoscope card of Niagara Falls, the American side.

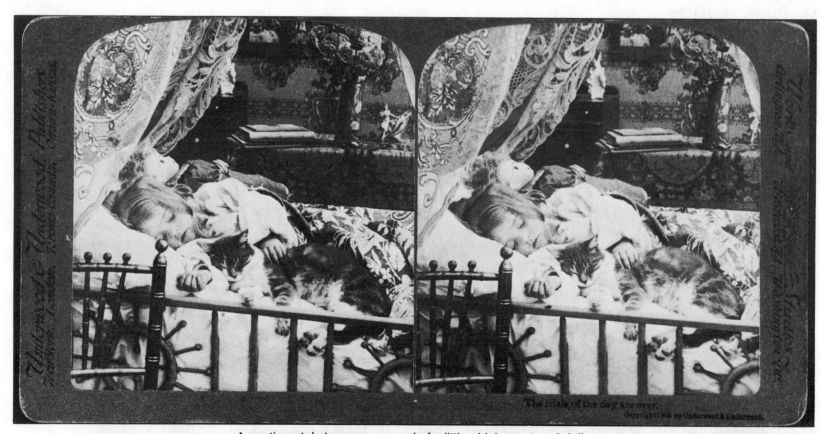

A sentimental stereoscope card of a little girl, her cat and doll.

Although stereoscopes declined in popularity after the 1850s, interest in them was revived during the 1890s and early 1900s. Mail-order houses such as Sears, Roebuck and Company of Chicago sold very cheap stereoscopes and huge collections of stereoscopic cards to thousands of people throughout the country.

Photography was opening up the world of faraway places and different experiences, as well as beginning to be used to record historical events. The Crimean War in Russia (1853-1856) and the American Civil War (1861-1865) established photography as an important means of communication between people and nations.

# STEREOSCOPES

24c

Advertisement from a 1908 Sears, Roebuck and Company catalogue.

Brady Staff. Portrait of Mathew B. Brady, Carte de visite, circa 1863. *Courtesy of the National Archives*

The most famous photographer of the Civil War was Mathew B. Brady. Before the War, Brady had established himself as a very successful daguerreotypist and carte de visite photographer. His portraits of famous people had made him very popular among the politicians.

In 1860, Brady took a photograph of Abraham Lincoln when he arrived at Cooper Union, a New York City college, to give a major campaign speech. The photograph showed a man of great dignity and inner strength. By the next day, both the speech and the photograph were famous. Woodcuts were made from the photograph to be used in newspapers and magazines. This may have been one of the first times that the publicity value of a photograph was recognized. Two years after his election, Lincoln claimed that the Brady photograph and the Cooper Union speech had made him President.

When the Civil War began in April 1861, Brady recognized the unique contribution that photography could make in documenting the battles and destruction of the War. He organized teams of photographers made up of men such as Alexander Gardner and Timothy O'Sullivan. They took pictures of privates and generals; land and sea battles; wounded and dead soldiers; prisons and hospitals; and of burned plantations and city ruins.

Brady and his teams were often in great danger as their photography wagons traveled through the military camps and onto the battlefields. They used the wet-plate collodion process in large cameras that required at least 10-second exposures. Even though action shots were impossible, their scenes of battlefields and ruins communicated the reality and horror of war to Americans throughout the country.

Mathew B. Brady. Cooper Union Lincoln portrait, 1860. *Courtesy of the Library of Congress*

Mathew B. Brady.  Ruins of Richmond, Virginia, 1865. The dark area in the lower right-hand corner is the result of damage to the original glass plate. *Courtesy of the National Archives*

Sometimes, Brady and the other photographers had the chance to pose their subjects so that their pictures were even more dramatic. For example, in the photograph of President Lincoln visiting General George McClellan at Antietam, Maryland, in 1862, Gardner arranged the scene so that Lincoln is the focus of attention. Lincoln is taller and is wearing his stovepipe hat. And, he is in the center, surrounded by the general and officers.

Alexander Gardner. President Lincoln visiting the battlefield at Antietam, Maryland, October 3, 1862. General McClellan and fifteen members of his staff are also in the photograph.
*Courtesy the National Archives*

Brady's famous portrait of General Sherman was formally posed. In fact, all of the pictures of soldiers had to be formal because of the exposure time required. There is still a lot that we can learn about the subject and the photographer, though, by looking closely at the photographs.

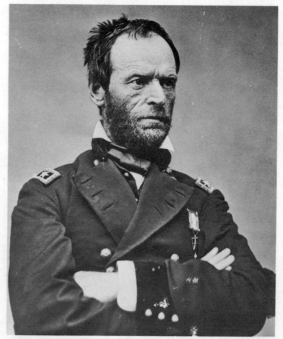

Mathew B. Brady's portrait of General William Sherman. *Courtesy of the National Archives*

In the Brady portrait, we see what Sherman looked like. We see his uniform, medals and the black sash tied around his arm in mourning for President Lincoln. We also can see that Sherman chose to have his picture taken with uncombed hair and untrimmed whiskers. He posed with his arms firmly crossed, staring away from the camera. Brady took the portrait against a plain background to create a strong, direct portrait.

After the Civil War, many men such as O'Sullivan and Gardner began photographing the American frontier. They took photographs of its unexplored regions and new towns. They also photographed native Americans, soldiers and settlers. These photographs gave people in the East a chance to see what the West really looked like and to see what life was like on the frontier.

An afternoon of croquet. Ladies, gentlemen and children on the lawn at Fort Bridger, Wyoming Territory, circa 1873. *Courtesy of the National Archives*

Many frontier photographers were hired by the railroad companies. People everywhere were fascinated with the progress of the transcontinental railroad and wanted to see pictures of its construction. Perhaps the most famous of all these photographs was taken when the rails finally met on May 10, 1869, at Promontory Point, Utah. The picture below shows the two engines very close to meeting. Construction superintendents, workers and celebrities are gathered on the tracks and engines to take part in the celebration.

Joining of the tracks for the first transcontinental railroad, Promontory Point, Utah Territory, 1869. *Courtesy of the National Archives*

O'Sullivan's photograph of his darkroom wagon crossing the sand dunes of Carson Desert, Nevada, 1867-69. *Courtesy of the National Archives*

The United States government also hired photographers as part of scientific expeditions to explore and survey the American frontier. O'Sullivan's experience as a wet-plate photographer under the dangerous and difficult circumstances of the War made him an ideal person for these expeditions. Turning a Civil War army ambulance wagon into a darkroom, he began traveling thousands of miles taking pictures. His photographs established a permanent record of what the West was like during the late 1860s and 1870s.

William Henry Jackson. *Photographing in High Places*. Tetons Range, 1872. *Courtesy of the National Archives*

**DARKROOM**
**A room in which photographic materials are processed, in either complete darkness or with a safelight.**

Both O'Sullivan and another famous photographer of the frontier, William Henry Jackson, were not only skilled technical photographers, but also daring men who experimented with new ways of seeing the world through photography.

Perhaps the most famous of all of these photographs is O'Sullivan's view of the Indian cliff dwellings in the Canon de Chelle, which were abandoned in the 1200s. Notice how careful he was to find the best spot from which to view the scene. He framed it on the plate to create a spectacular picture. O'Sullivan was also concerned with capturing light as it played against canyon walls. He used the light to record the spirit and mood of the landscape in his photograph.

The work of the early frontier photographers was not limited to landscapes. They also took pictures of the people who lived in the West. Wet-plate photographs of American Indians were not just portraits of people, but a record of a culture as well.

All of the wet-plate collodion photographs taken by men like Brady and O'Sullivan had to be exposed and processed before the collodion dried. Therefore, lots of equipment and a great deal of skill were needed by the photographer. It was necessary to carry a complete **darkroom** to the place where the pictures were to be taken. Tents and wagons became darkrooms where photographs could be developed. Since the wet-plate process required many different chemicals, a photographer's darkroom during the 1800s was really a very complete laboratory.

O'Sullivan. Distant view of Ancient Ruins in the lower part of Canon de Chelle, Arizona Territory, 1873. *Courtesy of the National Archives*

John K. Hilliers. *A Moki, weaving*, 1879. *Courtesy of the National Archives*

99

Photographer unknown. Portrait of unidentified Indians from Southeastern Idaho Reservation, 1897. *Courtesy of the National Archives*

By the 1870s, many different scientists and photographers were experimenting with possible ways to make dry plates. They did not want to have to carry a darkroom and trunk full of chemicals around everywhere they took pictures. Some of these inventors even tried to use beer, licorice and sugar to make a dry plate!

A photographer and an assistant with a darkroom set up in a tent.

A photographer fully equipped to take pictures in the wilderness.

In 1871, Dr. Richard L. Maddox, an English physician and photographer, discovered a dry-plate process by using warm gelatin instead of collodion. He mixed it with a few other chemicals to create the gelatin-bromide emulsion necessary for a successful dry-plate process. The emulsion was poured over a glass plate and allowed to dry. The plate could then be stored until exposed and did not have to be developed immediately.

Other photographers began experimenting with the process. By the 1880s, enough improvements had been made that many manufacturers began producing the dry plates. With this new process, photographers only had to carry a camera, a few loaded dry-plate holders and perhaps a tripod. The plates could be exposed wherever the picture was being taken and developed back in the photographer's darkroom when it was convenient. The exposure time required was also reduced so that less formal poses were possible. Photographers could even hold their cameras steady without having to use a tripod.

Once again, the science and art of photography was greatly changed. The dry-plate method made it much easier for a photographer to take pictures anywhere. They could be developed at any time in their own simplified darkroom with chemicals and equipment that they could easily buy from mail-order companies such as Sears, Roebuck and Company. This new method made it possible for both amateur and professional photographers to buy dry plates already manufactured from companies such as George Eastman's dry-plate factory in Rochester, New York. They could also send the exposed plates to a developing company to make the prints for them!

A photographer in his darkroom in the late 1880s.

In re-creating many of the experiments included in the rest of this book—such as developing your own photographs—you may find it fun and helpful to set up a simple darkroom of your own in a bathroom, garage or basement. Two things are required for making your own darkroom: one is total darkness; the other is ventilation. If you cannot set up a darkroom at home, you can still do all of the experiments and take your own photographs by having your film developed by a photography store or laboratory.

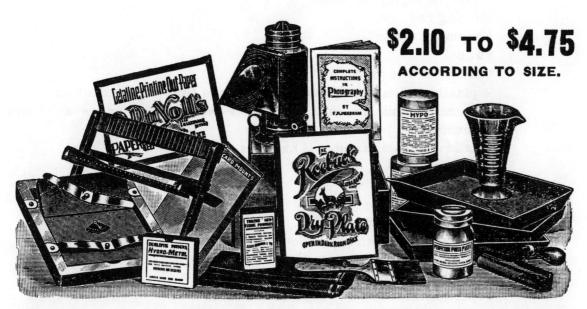

A developing, finishing and material outfit for either plate cameras or film cameras advertised in the Sears, Roebuck and Company catalogue for 1908.

In order to set up your own darkroom, you will need the following materials and supplies:

A small room that can be made totally dark (A windowless bathroom with a ceiling fan will work very well.)

Four 5″ x 7″ photographic trays, that are at least 1½″ deep, for chemicals

Large photographic tray measuring 18″ x 21″

Three photographic tongs

Stirring rod

Pitcher for water

Funnel

Graduated measuring cylinder

4 plastic-gallon jugs (Plastic gallon jugs that bleach, distilled water or milk come in, will work very well if they are washed out thoroughly.)

Plastic clothespins and coat hangers

Masking tape

An indelible marker

Scissors

Photographic thermometer

Watch or clock with a luminous dial

Safelight

Work board or surface

Paper towels

Overhead light

Flexible-neck electric lamp with a 100-watt bulb

Piece of glass, 8″ x 10″, with the edges taped

**Developer** for film
**Stop Bath** for film
**Fixer** for film
Box of resin-coated photographic paper
Developer for paper
Fixer for paper

Remove anything in your darkroom that might get in your way while working. Make sure that there is an electrical outlet close-by for your safelight and the overhead light. SINCE YOU WILL BE HANDLING CHEMICALS AND LIQUIDS, BE VERY CAREFUL NOT TO TOUCH THE OUTLETS WITH WET HANDS BECAUSE YOU COULD BE SHOCKED.

You can block out any light that might be leaking into the room by pushing towels under the cracks of the door or by taping over where light might be coming in.

If possible, buy a safelight with a clip-on bracket from a photography store. A safelight has special protective filters which allow enough light to be able to see in the dark, but not enough to expose the light-sensitive photographic paper or film you are working with. Place the light off to the side of the table where you are working. This way, the light will not damage the paper or film by shining too closely to them. If you do not want to use a clip-on safelight, you can buy a red-safelight bulb from a photography or hardware store and substitute it for the regular light bulb in the bathroom fixture.

**DEVELOPER**

A chemical used to make the image recorded on a photographic surface (plate, paper or film) visible.

**STOP BATH**

A chemical bath used to stop development by neutralizing unwanted developer remaining in the emulsion layer.

**FIXER**

A chemical used to wash away any unused emulsion on negatives and prints to prevent discoloration of the photographic surface and make the image permanent.

The most important part of your darkroom are the chemicals which you will use to develop your photographs. There are many different types of chemicals you can use. Preparing chemicals can be very confusing, since different photographic companies use varying names for similar products.

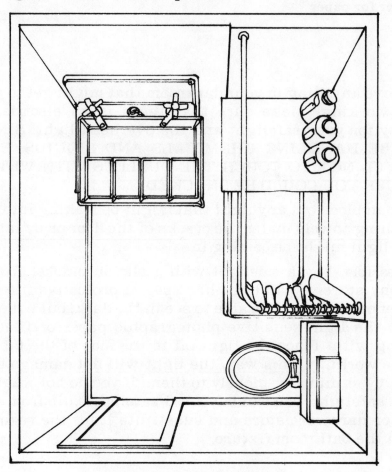

A bathroom turned into a darkroom.

The strengths needed to make film developer are different from those for paper developer. Instructions for mixing chemicals are different depending upon the manufacturer. Always follow the instructions included with the product you are using very carefully. The chemicals can be mixed in normal daylight.

Chemicals come in liquid concentrates and dry powders that must be mixed. Choose which form is the easiest for you to use. Liquid concentrates are generally easier to mix, but are not always as easy to find in photography stores as dry chemicals.

In order to process your own film and photographic paper for the experiments included in the rest of REDISCOVERING PHOTOGRAPHY, you will need to mix concentrations of film developer, photographic paper developer, stop bath and fixer.

All of the chemicals that you have mixed should be stored in a safe, dark and cool place. Make sure that you have tightened the lids on the plastic jugs and wiped the outside of the jugs clean. Clean up your work area. BE PARTICULARLY CAREFUL THAT YOU STORE YOUR CHEMICALS WHERE YOUNG CHILDREN CANNOT GET INTO THEM, SINCE ALL OF THE CHEMICALS THAT YOU HAVE MIXED ARE POISONOUS IF SWALLOWED.

You are now ready to develop and print your own photographs. Before you can do so, you will need to finish building your camera.

As you know from reading REDISCOVERING PHOTOGRAPHY up to this point, all of the basic elements of a photographic camera are included in your camera obscura. All that is needed in order to take a photograph is a lightproof back for the camera, a method for holding the film in place and a mechanical-shutter system.

Cut out the patterns for the camera back included on pages 112 and 113. Assemble them as illustrated below.

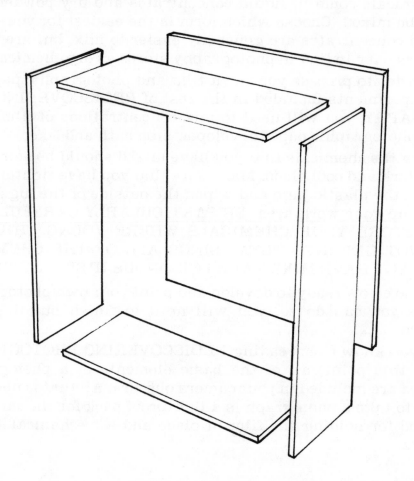

**Glue the pieces together.**

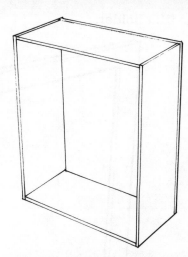

If you have assembled the camera back properly, it should fit snugly over the back of the camera body and come to rest against the accessory stop.

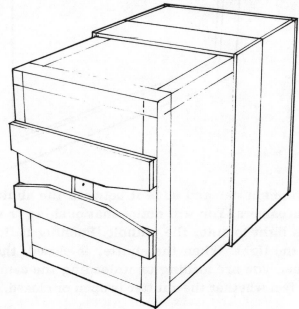

**Cut out the film holder.**

Cut out the shutter and slide it between the shutter brackets and the front of the camera. You will notice that pushing the shutter flush to one side allows light to enter the pinhole. Pushing it flush to the other side closes off the light. When the shutter is closed, the notched portion is visible. When you are loading or unloading the camera in the dark, you can tell by feel whether the shutter is open or closed.

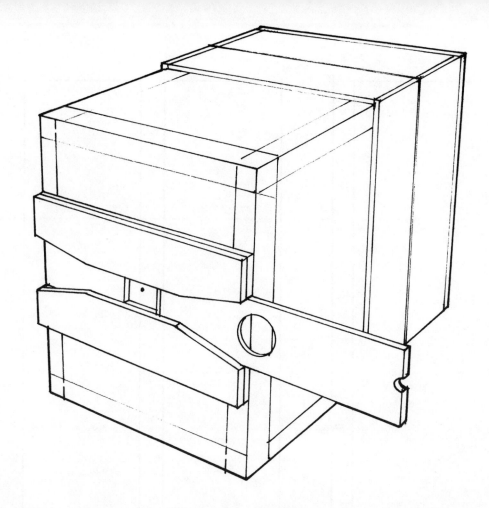

You are now ready to make your own photographs. Take the camera and a piece of 4″ x 5″ photographic paper into a completely dark room. Always be careful that the photographic paper is not exposed to the light.

You may find it helpful to practice putting a 4″ x 5″ piece of paper into the camera before you actually do it with photographic paper in the dark.

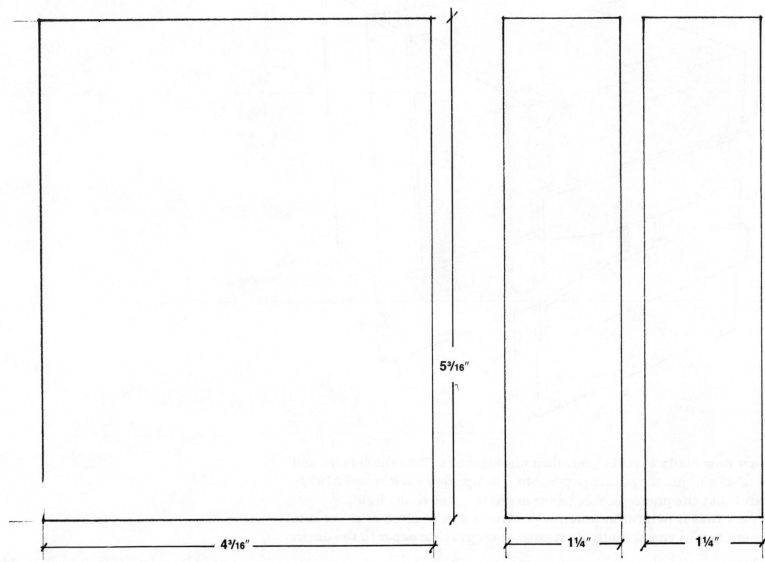

5³/₁₆″

4³/₁₆″

1¼″

1¼″

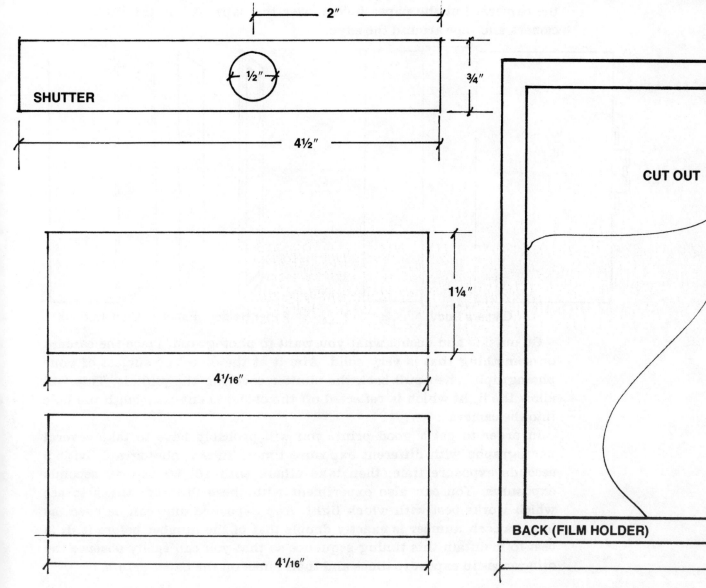

SHUTTER

2″

½″

¾″

4½″

1¼″

4¹/₁₆″

4¹/₁₆″

CUT OUT

BACK (FILM HOLDER)

4″

Place the photographic paper, emulsion or shiny side up, in the back of the camera. Put the paper holder over the paper. Close the back of the camera and tape around the edge.

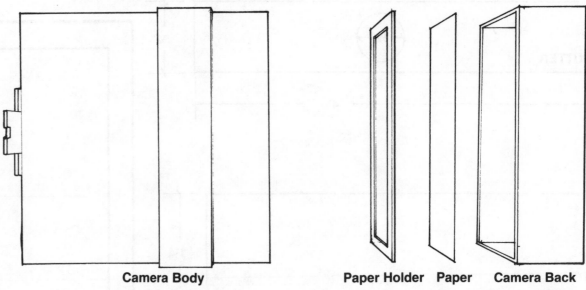

Camera Body      Paper Holder   Paper    Camera Back

Go outside and decide what you want to photograph. Place the camera on something that is very solid. Aim it at the object or subject of your photograph. Then pull back the shutter covering the pinhole. This will allow the light which is reflected off the object to enter through the hole into the camera.

In order to get a good print, you will probably have to take several photographs with different exposure times. Take a photograph with 5 seconds exposure time, then take others with 10, 20 and 40 seconds exposures. You can also experiment with these different times to see which works best with which light. Any exposure time can be used, as long as each number is exactly double that of the number before it. It is best to maintain this timing sequence so that you can easily observe the differences in exposure times and their effect on the paper prints.

As you know, light exposes the film in a camera. If a camera has a lens system for focusing, then the light is controlled by the size of the aperture opening in relation to the amount of time that the shutter is open. The greater the lens opening, the faster the shutter speed; the smaller the lens opening, the slower the shutter speed. The settings for these openings on modern cameras are called f-stops.

The lower the f-stop number, the greater the opening. Thus, F-2 is the largest opening and F-16 is the smallest. Lower f-stops allow faster shots and tend to eliminate focusing problems when you hold the camera by hand.

Another use for f-stops is to increase or decrease the depth of field, or the amount of space in front of the camera that is in focus. You can see how this works by squinting your eyes and looking at an object across the room. By squinting, you are in fact stopping down your own eyes to increase the depth of field. So, the higher the f-stop, the greater the depth of field.

You will find that it is very important to keep a record of each exposure time for your paper and film negatives. You may find it easiest to keep this information, along with notes on the lighting conditions under which you took your negatives, in a notebook.

Your negatives may be stored in glassine envelopes or sleeves, which can be bought inexpensively at most photography stores. It is all right to write the exposure times on the glassines, but never write it on the negative itself.

In order to set up your darkroom for printing and developing the negatives you have taken, place the large tray over the top of the sink. Make sure that it can sit there safely. Using the indelible marker, carefully print "DEV" for developer, "STOP" for stop bath and "FIX" for fixer separately on a 4" x 5" tray. Place these trays inside the large tray along with a fourth tray for washing. Mark "WATER" on the fourth tray.

Always set up the trays in the following order: "DEV," "STOP," "FIX" and "WATER." Try to get into the habit of always working each step of the process toward the washing or last try. This is the standard way you should set up your chemical trays when working in your darkroom. Make sure that all of your containers and tools are clean.

Pour 10 ounces of the full-strength paper developer into the graduated-measuring cylinder. BE VERY CAREFUL NOT TO SPLASH.

By mixing hot and cold water together, bring a pitcher of water down to 68° F. A good way to bring the water temperature down is to put an ice cube in a plastic bag and lower it into the water. Then add 20 ounces of the water to the paper developer in the graduated-measuring cylinder. Pour the diluted paper developer into the tray marked "DEV."

Next, pour enough stop bath into the "STOP" tray to cover the bottom about 1″ deep. If you are using concentrated stop bath, use 2 ounces stop bath for each gallon of water.

Do the same with the paper fixer in the tray marked "FIX."

Set out a pair of tongs in front of each of the chemical trays. In order not to confuse them, you may find it helpful to label each pair of tongs with the indelible pen and masking tape according to the tray each pair will be used with.

In order to develop your photograph, turn off the overhead light in your darkroom. Switch on the safelight. Remove the piece of photographic paper from the back of the camera or its light-safe storage envelope and place it, emulsion or shiny side up, in the tray marked "DEV."

Make sure that the piece of photographic paper is completely covered by the developer. If it is not completely submerged, gently push it down with the tongs. Leave the paper in the developer until you see a picture clearly develop. This usually takes about one minute.

Once your photograph has fully developed, lift it out of the developer with the proper tongs. Hold the photograph over the tray with the tongs and gently shake off any excess developer.

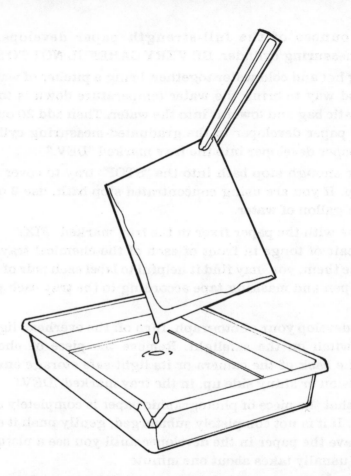

Set the photograph in the tray of stop bath for 15 seconds and agitate it or move it back and forth. Using the stop-bath tongs, lift the photograph out of the tray and shake off the excess chemicals.

Set the photograph in the tray of fixer. If you are using glossy photographic paper, it should remain in the fixer for 45 seconds. If you are using resin-coated paper, it should remain for 2 minutes. Always follow the instructions included with the product you are using.

Using the fixer tongs, lift the photograph out of the tray and set it in the "WATER" tray in order to wash the photograph.

When you have a number of prints to wash, it will probably be most convenient for you to set the water tray under a faucet. The bathtub is good for this step. Let the water run over the tray and down the drain. You may wish to buy a washing tray which has holes on one of its ends to let the water run out of it. Cold water is best with a temperature of about 65° to 75° F. Let your print wash from between 30 to 60 minutes. Be sure to check the instructions for the product you are using. Remove the print from the water and let it dry by hanging it on a clothesline or coat hanger with a plastic clip.

You have made a negative-paper print. In it, black and white are reversed. In order to make a positive print of your negative photograph:

1. Return to the darkroom.
2. In total darkness, place a piece of photographic paper on the table, emulsion side up.
3. Position your negative print directly over the piece of paper, image side down.
4. Cover the two pieces of paper with the piece of glass.
5. Turn on the overhead white light for 10 seconds. If this is not enough time, double the exposure to 20 seconds, 40 seconds, etc., until you get an image.
6. Develop, stop, fix and wash the print as you did to make the negative-paper print.

Basically, you have just reproduced the method used by Fox Talbot during the late 1830s and early 1840s to print positive prints. As was the case with Talbot, the negative that you have made is probably somewhat fuzzy.

You will be able to take clearer pictures if you use film rather than photographic paper. Load your camera with 4″ x 5″ sheets of negative film instead of the sheets of photographic paper. This type of film is available at most photography stores. Ask for the slowest-speed film available, which is better for taking long exposures.

When you are taking photographs with your pinhole camera, you may find it awkward to come back into your darkroom every time you need to change the piece of paper or film. You can solve this problem by making a simple changing bag to carry along with you wherever you want to take photographs.

**In order to make the changing bag you will need:**
    **A large, heavy-duty, black plastic garbage bag**
    **Scissors**
    **Black masking tape or electrician's tape**
    **2 large rubber bands**

**Place the bag on a flat surface as shown below.**

**Cut the bag down the middle for about 2/3 its length.**

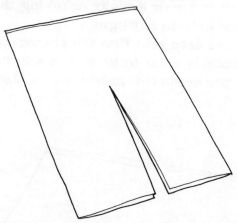

Roll the inside edges back and tape them securely as shown. Make sure that the hole in one of the arms of the bag is large enough for your camera to fit inside the bag through the hole.

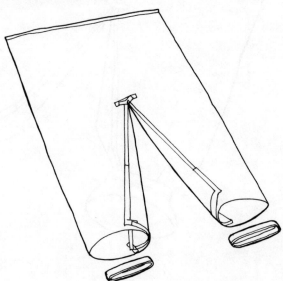

Place the rubber bands over the ends of the arm openings to seal them. When you are putting your arms in or taking them out of the changing bag, be careful not to let in any light.

Although you can keep your film and photographic paper in the changing bag, it is probably safer to keep it in a light-safe container. An old photographic paper or sheet-film box with a black-paper liner will work very well.

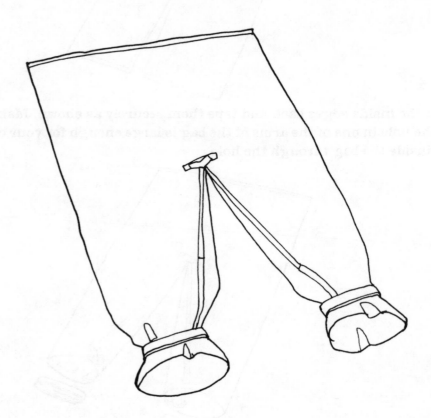

Now go outside and take a couple of photographs. Try different exposure times. As with the photographic paper, always double exposure time for each picture, until you find the one that works best with the light you have.

Return to your darkroom after you have taken your photograph on film. Set up the same equipment in exactly the same way that you did for developing your paper print. Make sure that all of your equipment is clean.

In developing your film, you will use film developer in place of paper developer. You can use the same fixer and stop bath for either process.

Usually film is professionally developed in a special type of holder. Instead, you can develop your film in trays in much the same way as it was done in the 1800s.

Carefully read the instructions on developing included with your film. Be sure to check the time sequences listed for each step.

---

Hold the film at its edge with the developer tongs and set it in the developer tray. Gently move the film back and forth for the amount of time suggested by the manufacturer of the film.

Lift the film out of the developer and shake off any excess. Place the film in the stop bath for 15 seconds.

Using the stop-bath tongs, transfer the film to the fixer tray. Leave the film in the fixer for at least four minutes.

Remove the film from the fixer with the fixer tongs and wash it in the washing tray with running water for at least 30 to 45 minutes.

Hang the film up to dry with the plastic clips on a clothesline or coat hanger.

**CONTACT PRINT**

A positive photographic print made by printing from a paper or film negative placed directly on its surface.

In order to make your own **contact prints** from the negative film, you will need to set up the chemicals and equipment in your darkroom in exactly the same way you did for making the positive print.

The only additional equipment necessary will be a 5½" x 4¼" piece of very clean glass. Tape it around the edges. A 100-watt electric lamp with a flexible neck will also be used. Be sure that your working surface is flat and away from chemicals and water. A card table would work well, or you could put a board on the floor.

Place a piece of photographic paper on top of the flat surface, emulsion (or shiny) side up. Put your negative, shiny side down, over the piece of paper. Place the glass on top of the paper and the negative.

Set the light 12 to 15 inches above the piece of glass. Turn on the light for about 15 seconds. Take the piece of photographic paper out from under the glass. Store the negative in a safe place.

Develop, stop and fix the piece of paper in exactly the same way that you did your negative print. If you exposed the paper properly, you should have a very good positive print. If the photograph is underexposed or overexposed, experiment with leaving the light on for either longer or shorter periods of time.

The manufacture of dry plates and the establishment of companies that developed and fixed photographs made photography enjoyable for many more men, women and children across the country. Shorter-exposure times and faster shutters resulted in the development of smaller, handheld cameras. Everywhere, people were trying to take candid photographs of their friends and family. It was often considered bad manners to ask someone if you could take their picture. For this reason, many small cameras became known as "detective" cameras. They were hidden in all sorts of ways—in a derby hat, a vest, a pistol, a book, or even in a cane. Naturally, the lenses and shutters of these cameras had to be very cleverly disguised and operated.

George Eastman, one of the pioneer manufacturers of gelatin dry plates, believed that the process of taking pictures could be made even easier. At first, his experiments focused on eliminating the heavy, awkward dry plates. By coating a roll of paper with two layers of chemically treated gelatin, he discovered how to successfully produce a flexible roll of film. It became known as American film.

A detective camera in a watch, 1887.

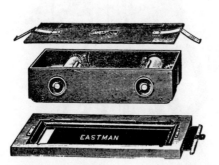

Interior and slide front of the roll holder.

A photograph taken of George Eastman in 1884 by an unknown photographer. Eastman wrote on the print that it was made on his new gelatin-coated paper film. *Courtesy George Eastman House, Rochester*

Eastman continued experimenting with the film until he was able to replace the paper with transparent plastic. It was this development which gave birth to modern-photographic film.

The new rolls of film had to somehow be held in position in the camera though. So Eastman and William H. Walker, a camera maker who had joined his company, invented a roll holder. It could be fitted into any standard-plate camera.

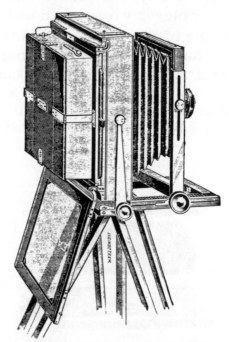

Eastman camera with a roll holder attached.

Still not satisfied with the cameras available, Eastman continued building improved models. In March 1888, he was able to patent a small box camera with a roll holder for film. It became the basis for all modern cameras. He named the camera Kodak. It measured 6″ x 3½″ x 4″ and took 100 exposures on one roll of film.

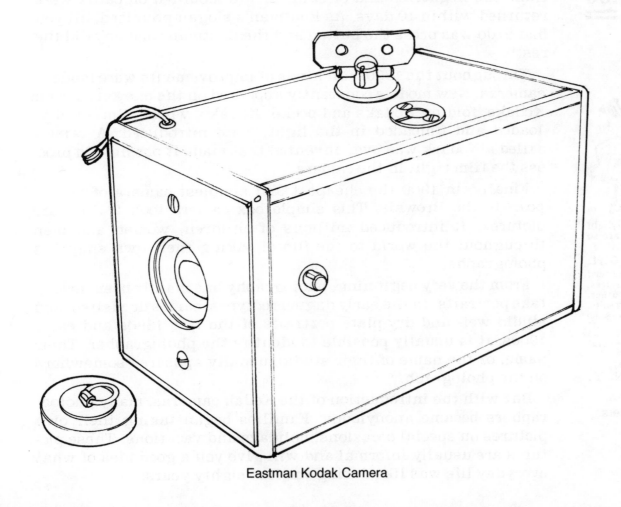

**Eastman Kodak Camera**

An early advertisement for Brownie cameras.

For the first time, complete developing and printing services came with the camera. You bought it loaded with a roll of film. When you finished taking 100 exposures, you mailed the camera, still loaded with the film, back to Eastman's factory. The camera was returned immediately, loaded with a new unexposed roll of film. The negatives and circular prints mounted on cards were returned within 10 days. As Eastman's slogan promised, all you had to do was press the button and the Eastman company did the rest!

Throughout the 1890s, all kinds of improvements were made in cameras. New models constantly appeared on the market. Larger Kodaks, folding Kodaks and pocket Kodaks, whose film could be loaded and unloaded in the light, were introduced. A camera called a Nodark was even invented that made it possible to process the film right in the camera.

Finally, in 1900 the cheapest and simplest camera of all appeared—the Brownie. This simple box camera took 2¼" square pictures. It introduced millions of children, women and men throughout the world to the fun of taking their own snapshot photographs.

From the very beginning, photography has mainly been used to take portraits. In the early daguerreotypes, cartes de visites, and studio wet- and dry-plate portraits of the late 1890s and early 1900s, it is usually possible to identify the photographer. Their name, or the name of their studio, usually appeared somewhere on the photograph.

But with the introduction of the Kodak cameras, many photographers became anonymous. Families began taking their own pictures on special occasions, holidays and vacations. These pictures are usually informal and will give you a good idea of what everyday life was like during the last eighty years.

You may find it fun to look through your own family picture albums. See what sort of records you have of different members of your family, of their homes and of the places they have been. If you look closely at the photographs' shapes and sizes, you may also discover what types of cameras your family used.

Inventors, scientists and photographers all over the world have been experimenting with improvements in cameras, plates, films and the developing process itself throughout the history of photography. Many times they learned about each other's work and were able to pick up ideas that helped their own experiments succeed. These are the types of connections that often make great inventions possible. Usually the final solution is possible because many different people have worked on the smaller parts of a problem. Then someone fits the pieces of the puzzle together and solves the big problem.

For example, when Daguerre's discovery was made public, an Austrian professor, Andreas von Ettinghausen, realized that improvements needed to be made in Daguerre's lens. He worked on this problem with a colleague of his, Josef Max Petzval. They successfully designed a lens that would allow 16 times as much light into the camera as Daguerre's. Thus, the exposure time was reduced to less than a minute. Petzval's lens became known as the German lens and was used around the world for over 60 years. over 60 years.

In watching other people take photographs, you have probably seen them use different types of cameras. They may also have used different types of lenses depending upon their subject and the type of photograph they wanted to take. The lens is the most important part of the camera. A camera with a lens will produce a sharper image than the pinhole camera. The lens will also admit just enough light to take pictures with much quicker exposure

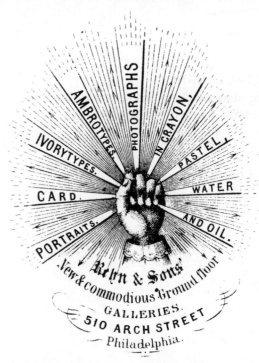

A photographer's advertisement on the back of a carte de visite photograph.

times. It is even possible to hold a camera with a lens and take an unblurred photograph of a moving subject.

Most modern cameras use a version of a convex lens of normal **focal length** that works very much like the human eye. Sometimes though, a photographer wants to control the size of the image in the photograph. This can be done in two ways. The camera can be moved itself, or the lens can be changed. With a thicker, more curved convex lens, the light rays are bent more sharply because they hit the lens at a sharper angle. This causes the light rays to meet just a short distance from the lens and to produce a smaller image.

**FOCAL LENGTH**
**The distance from the center of the lens to the focal plane of the camera.**

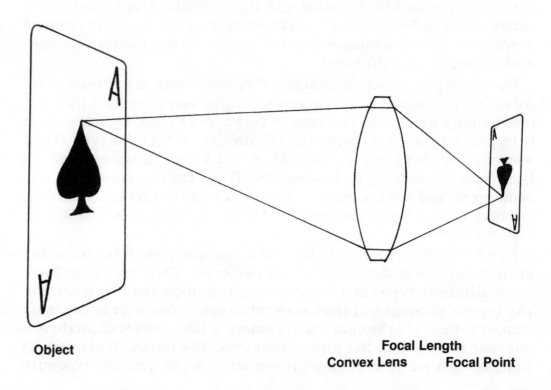

**Object**

**Convex Lens**

**Focal Length**

**Focal Point**

130

When a thinner, less curved convex lens is used, the rays of light do not meet until they are much further from the lens. This longer focal length creates a much larger image than the thicker lens did.

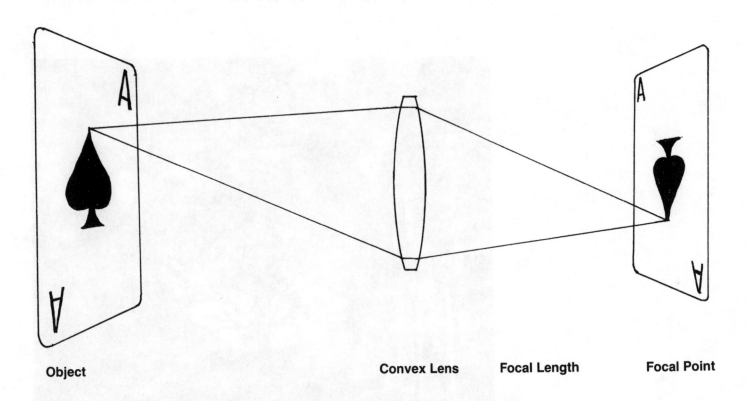

**Object**  **Convex Lens**  **Focal Length**  **Focal Point**

The pinhole camera you have made will take normal pictures as it is now made. However, by making a few simple modifications, you can also use your camera to take two other types of photographs. These require two different types of lenses, the wide-angle and the long-focus lens.

131

A wide-angle lens has a short focal length. It produces a smaller image. It is also able to get about 50 percent more of the subject onto the film than the eye can see because it takes in a wide angle of vision. By using this type of lens, a photographer can be very close to the object and yet capture all of it in the photograph.

**Wide-angle photograph taken with the Pinhole Camera described in this book.**

If you were to take a photograph of the ace of spades with the regular pinhole camera, you would have a picture that looks like this.

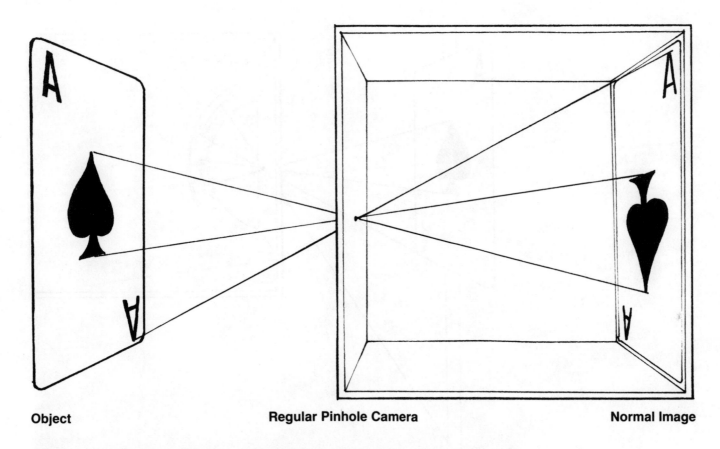

**Object**            **Regular Pinhole Camera**           **Normal Image**

With a wide-angle lens, the image becomes more narrowly focused. The curved back of the film-plane attachment for your camera compresses the focal plane where the image is projected much like a wide-angle lens does in a modern camera.

133

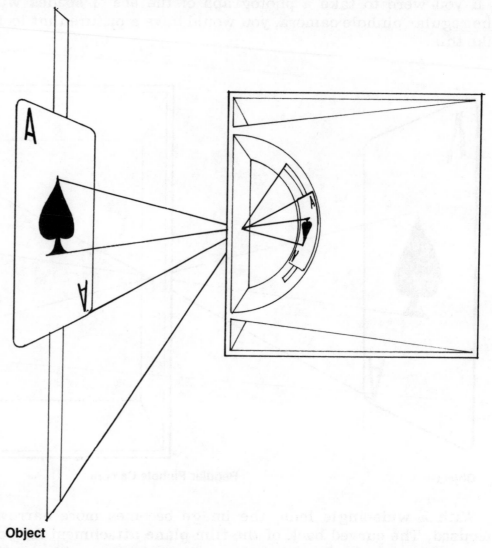

**Object**

Curved back film plane which compresses the focal plane where the wide-angle image is projected in the pinhole camera.

You can make an attachment for taking wide-angle photographs that will fit onto your pinhole camera. All you will need is a 20″ x 30″ sheet of ¹/₁₆″-thick cardboard and the other supplies you used to assemble the body of the pinhole camera.

Cut out the patterns for the wide-angle attachment on pages 140 through 142. Be sure to make a left and right side and a left and right film-plane support, even though there is only one pattern piece for each of these parts.

Assemble the 2 sides, top and bottom, as shown below. Glue the pieces together.

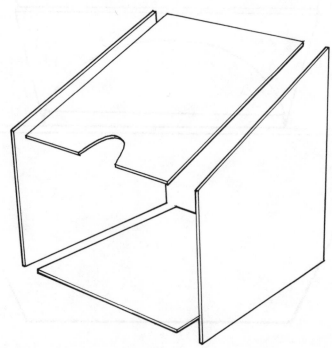

**Glue the two film-plane supports, opposite one another, on the inside of the attachment body as illustrated.**

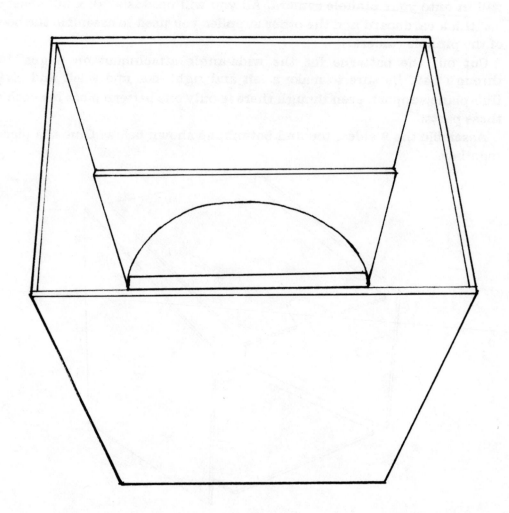

Carefully bend the film plane and glue it to the film-plane supports.

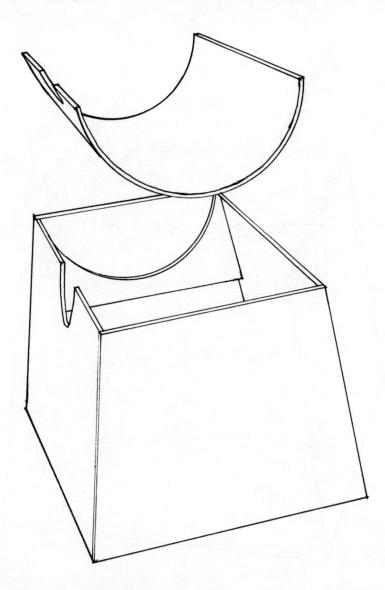

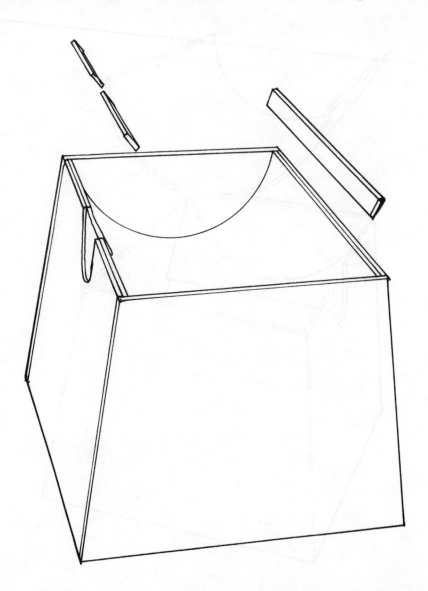

**Your wide-angle attachment is now complete and should look like this.**

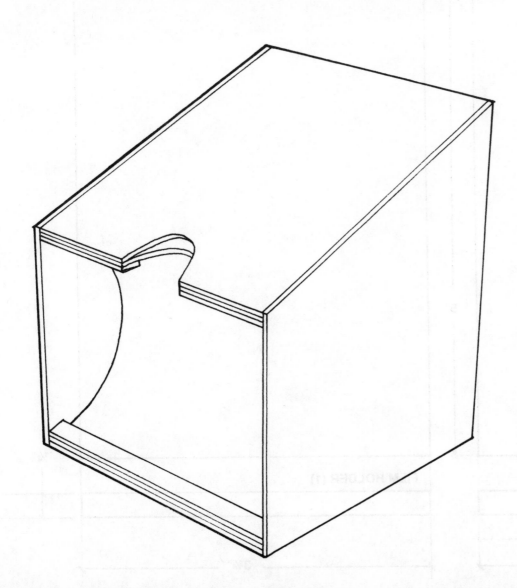

**WIDE-ANGLE ATTACHMENT PATTERNS**

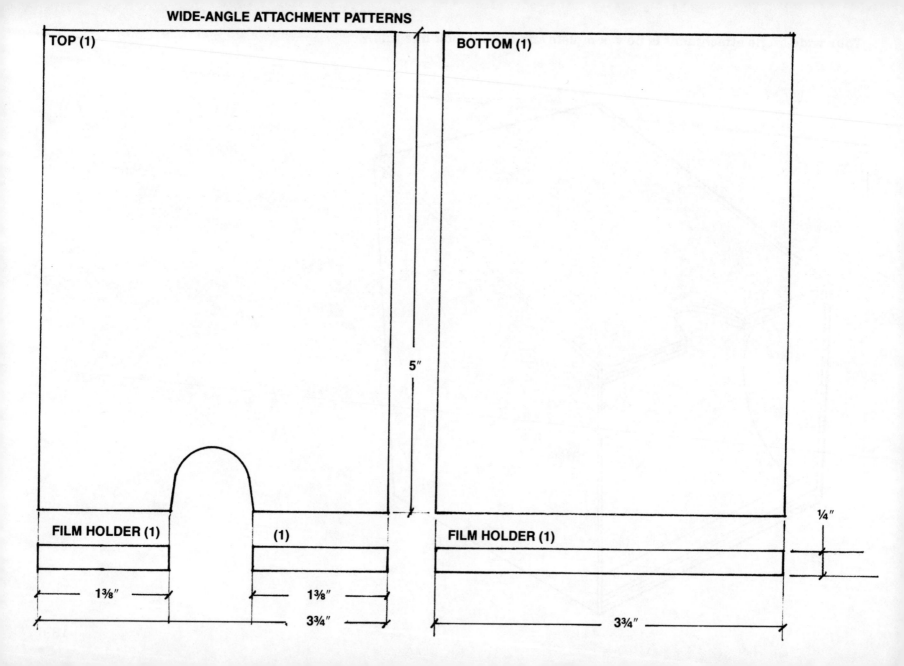

TOP (1)

BOTTOM (1)

5″

¼″

FILM HOLDER (1)

(1)

FILM HOLDER (1)

1⅜″

1⅜″

3¾″

3¾″

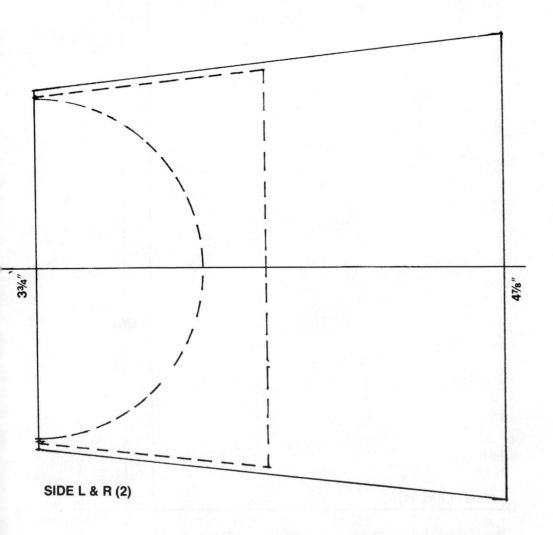

SIDE L & R (2)

3³⁄₄"

4⁷⁄₈"

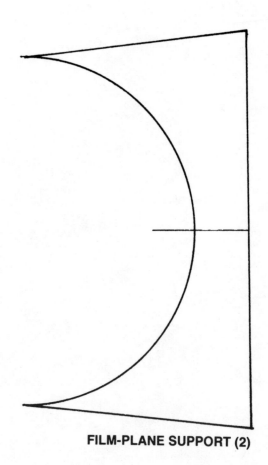

FILM-PLANE SUPPORT (2)

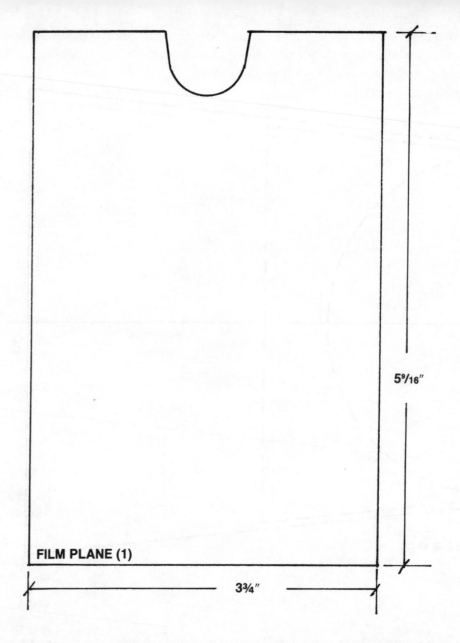

**FILM PLANE (1)**

5⁹/₁₆″

3¾″

In order to load your camera to take wide-angle photographs, place the film onto the curved film plane. You will have to trim the film with scissors so that it will fit on the film plane. Then fit the wide-angle attachment inside the back of the main body of the camera as shown below. Finally, put the back of the camera on and tape the seams.

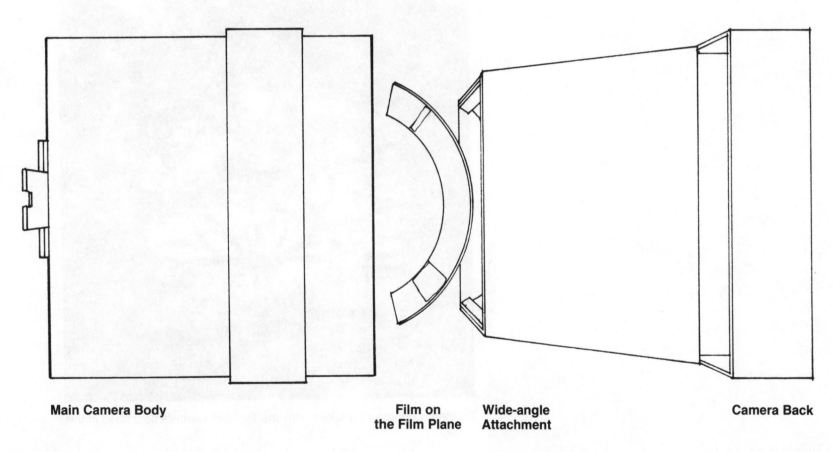

**Main Camera Body**

**Film on the Film Plane**

**Wide-angle Attachment**

**Camera Back**

A long-focus lens has a long focal length. It is called a telephoto lens because it acts like a telescope, providing a magnified image of a faraway object. When taking photographs of people, this type of lens lets the photographer stay far away so that the subjects are more relaxed as their picture is being taken.

Telephoto photograph taken with the Pinhole Camera described in this book.

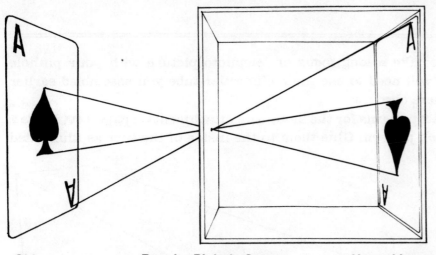

**Object**  **Regular Pinhole Camera**  **Normal Image**

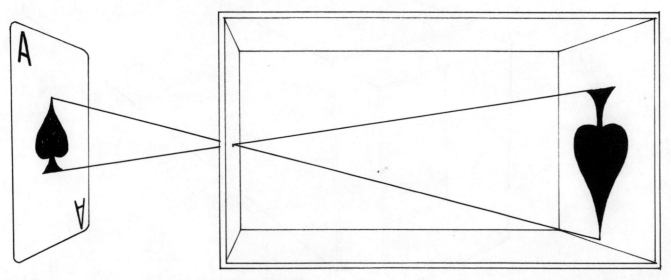

**Object**  **Telephoto Pinhole Camera**  **Long-focus Image**

In order to take a long-focus or telephoto picture with your pinhole camera, you will need to use the rectangular tube you assembled earlier for your camera obscura.

Cut out the 2 patterns for the mounting attachment on page 147. Make 2 pieces for each pattern. Glue them to the inside of the tube as illustrated below.

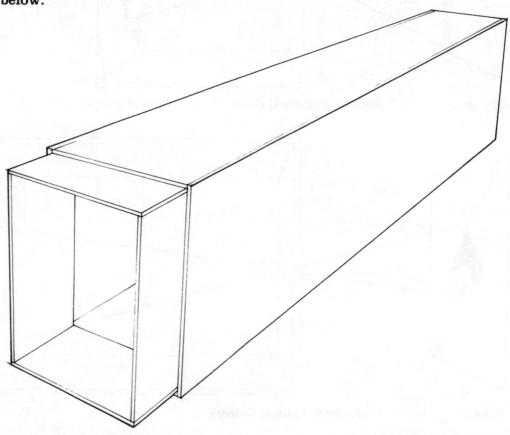

Attach the long tube to the back of your camera body. Replace the camera back and film holder on the back of the long tube in the same way you have already done on the regular pinhole camera.

## LONG LENS ATTACHMENT PATTERN

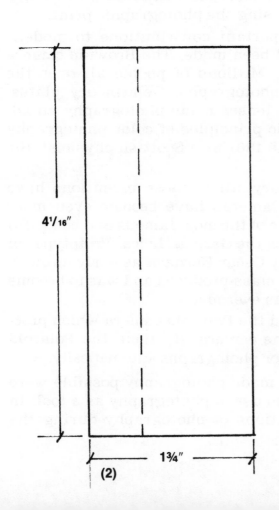

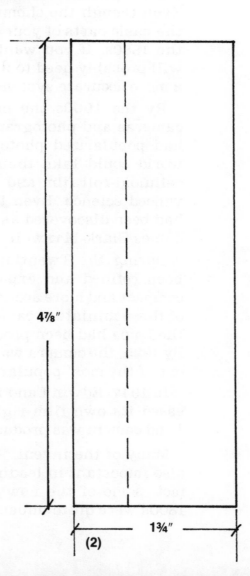

4¹/₁₆″

1¾″

(2)

4⅞″

1¾″

(2)

All types of photographic experiments are possible with your different camera attachments. For example, you could place the wide-angle device in the back of the telephoto lens attachment! Even though the chemistry and film you are using are modern, the basic parts of your camera are the same as they were during the 1880s. If you want to continue studying photography, you will probably need to invest in a more modern camera which has a more accurate system of exposing the photographic print.

By the 1900s the most important contributions to modern cameras and photography had been made. The Brownie camera had popularized photography. Millions of people all over the world could take their own photographs. Gelatin dry plates, celluloid-roll film and refined lenses made photography an advanced science. Even the basic principles of color photography had been discovered as early as 1861 by a Scottish physicist, Sir James Clark-Maxwell.

During the Twentieth Century, all of these inventions have been refined and expanded. Cameras have become even more compact and more accurate. One of the most famous and beautiful of these miniature cameras was the German Leica. Prototypes of the Leica had been produced by Oscar Barnack as early as 1913. By 1925, the camera was being mass-produced and was to become one of the most popular cameras ever made.

In 1947, Edwin Land invented the Polaroid camera which processed its own film right in the camera. By 1963, the Polaroid Land camera was producing color photographs automatically.

Many of the inventions that made photography possible were also important in leading to the use of photography as a tool. In fact, some of the new applications of photography during the 1800s were quite unusual.

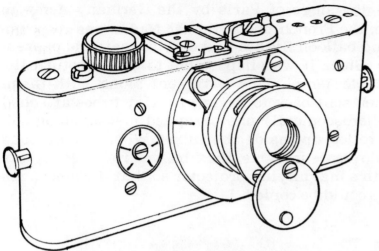

**The prototype German Leica camera.**

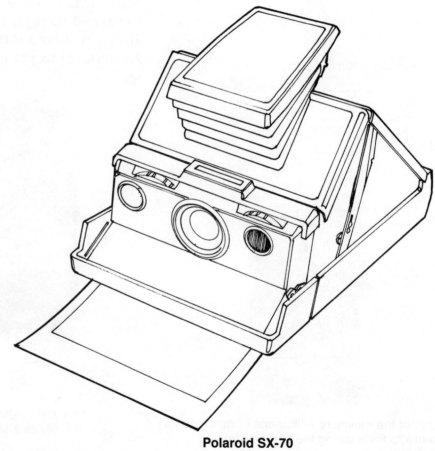

**Polaroid SX-70**

**NADAR**
**A pseudonym for the French artist and photographer, Gaspard Felix Tournachon.**

During the 131-day siege of Paris by the Germany Army in 1870, for example, the French photographer **Nadar** was responsible for establishing balloon flights that carried mail and passengers out of Paris. Since it was impossible to safely return the balloons to Paris, carrier pigeons were sent along with them. The birds were then sent back to Paris with tiny tubes attached to their wings. Microscopically photographed messages on collodion film were rolled up inside the tubes. When the pigeons returned to their dovecote in Paris, the film was removed. It was then projected with a magnifying projector so that the messages from outside Paris could be copied.

A carrier pigeon with tube to carry miniature pieces of collodion-film messages attached to its wing.

One of the miniature collections of messages sent into Paris during the 131-day siege.

Projecting and copying the microfilm messages brought by the carrier pigeons during the siege of Paris in 1870.

Basically, the same process of miniaturization is used today to make microfiche and microfilm. These forms of photography provide us with an inexpensive means of copying printed materials. Newspapers, books and business records can be stored in compact form. In fact, 164 pages of a typical book can be stored on a single microfiche card that measures only 5″ x 7″.

Martian Panorama. Taken from the Viking Lander when it landed on the surface of Mars, 1976.

When combined with new scientific instruments, photography has provided us with remarkable new ways of looking at the world. In our own time, photographs have made it possible to see the surface of Mars, the eye of a honeybee or the splash of a single drop of milk.

*Courtesy of the National Aeronautics and Space Administration*

David Scharf. *Honeybee's Eye.* Compound eye magnified 280 times. Photograph taken with a scanning electron microscope.

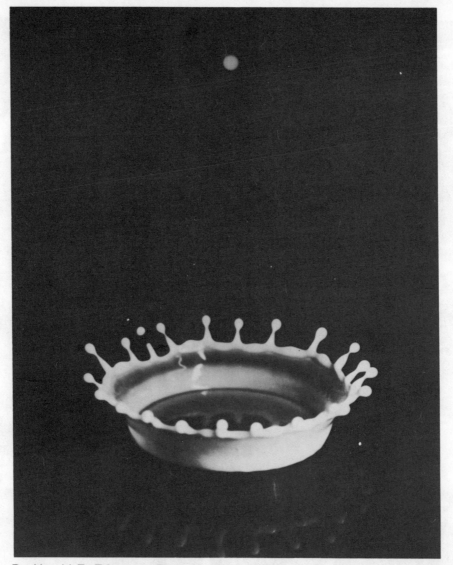

Dr. Harold E. Edgerton. Drop of milk splashing into a saucer, 1938. High-speed stroboscopic photography at 6,000 flashes per second.

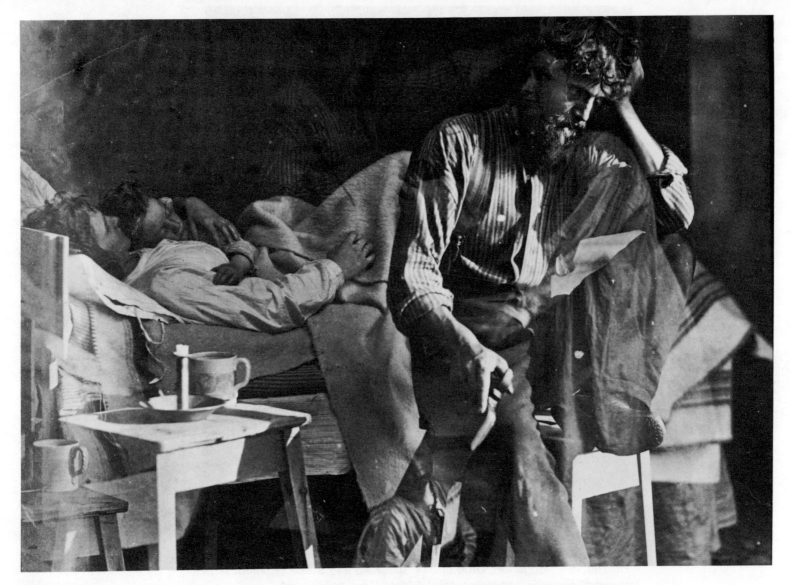

Oscar J. Rejlander. *Hard Times*. A spiritualistic photograph. *Courtesy George Eastman House, Rochester*

Just as photography has made it possible for us to understand and see the world in new ways, it has also provided us with a new way to express ourselves artistically. Beginning almost immediately with the discovery of photography during the 1800s, artists experimented with creating beautiful images through photography.

In the mid-1800s, the Swedish artist and photographer Oscar J. Rejlander experimented with superimposing photographic images. Rejlander used the wet-plate collodion process to create carefully posed pictures. Not only did he superimpose one negative over another, but sometimes he even painted special effects onto the negative. By doing this, Rejlander created multiple images in much the same way he would have created a painting.

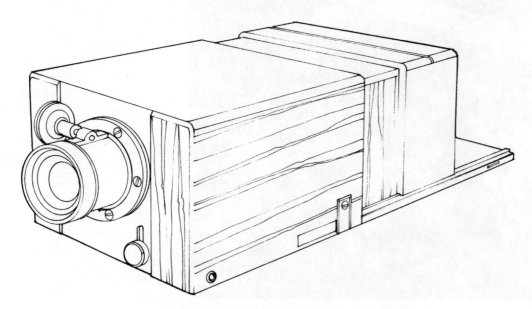

A wet-plate field camera from the 1850s.

Alfred Steiglitlz. *Steerage*, 1907. *Courtesy of the Library of Congress*

Photographers, such as American Alfred Steiglitz, used their cameras to explore familiar subjects in beautiful, suggestive ways. More interested in creating beautiful·photographs than imitation paintings, Steiglitz took what are known as "straight" photographs.

One of his most famous photographs, **The Steerage,** was taken on a European voyage in 1907. It is a picture of the lowest-paying passengers being herded into the steerage of the ship. Steiglitz believed that it was a great photograph because it combined human feelings with an interplay of shapes. Shapes such as the white drawbridge and the stairway, or the white straw hat and another man's white suspenders, are all related to one another. In this way, the picture is a photographic expression created by the photographer. It symbolizes rather than records human emotions and values.

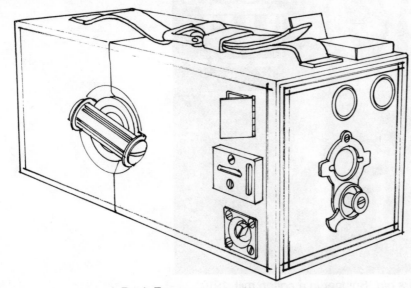

A Beck Frena, a magazine camera, 1892.

Lewis Hine. *Addie Laird, 12 years old.* Spinner in a cotton mill, 1910.
*Courtesy of the National Archives*

Sometimes, the photographer has had the opportunity to combine art and documentation. The photographs of Lewis Hine, for example, are not only strikingly historical documents, but beautiful and expressive artistic statements as well.

Hine used his photographs to tell his story of human situations. While working for the National Child Labor Committee in 1908, Hine took photographs of children working. He felt the photos would reveal the evils of child labor in the United States to the millions of people who read the magazines and newspapers where his photographs were published.

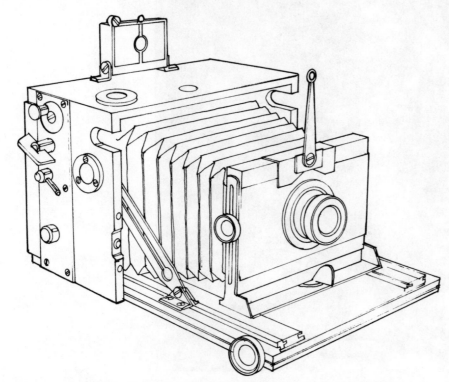

A Takir, E. Kraoss plate camera made in Paris in 1902.

Dorothea Lange. *California*, 1936. *Courtesy of the Library of Congress*

In much the same way, the documentary photographs of Dorothea Lange are powerful records of the Great Depression of the 1930s, as well as beautiful photographs.

While Lange was serving as a photographer for the Farm Security Administration, she took photographs—like the one of the California migrant mother and her children—that form a permanent record of a period in our history. Like Hine, Lange was aware of the great power her photographs had to influence public opinion about human conditions throughout the world.

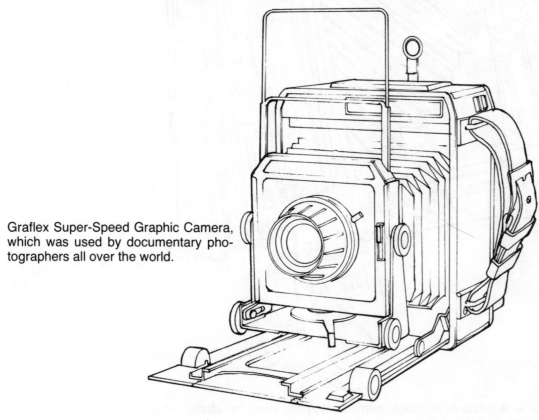

Graflex Super-Speed Graphic Camera, which was used by documentary photographers all over the world.

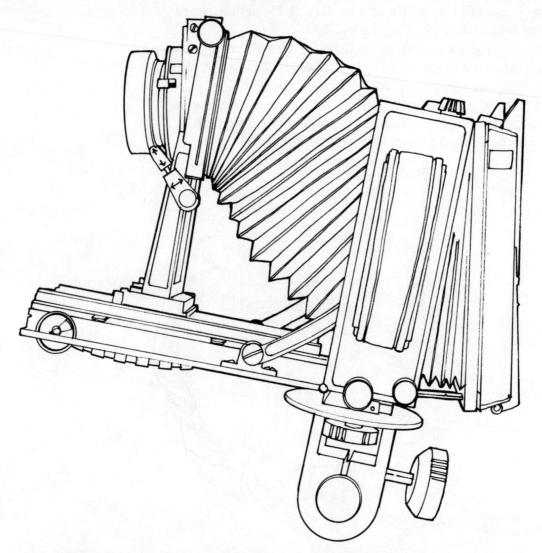

Linhof Super Technika V. A monorail technical camera, typically used for studio work including some indoor fashion photography.

In our own time, newspapers and magazines have come to rely on photographs to crowd more drama onto a page than is possible with just the printed word. Moments of great historical importance, personal happiness and suffering are captured in these photographs and shared with millions of readers.

Newspapers and magazines also rely on photographs for advertisements. For example, since the 1940s the world of fashion has depended on fashion photographers to sell their clothes. Striking poses, unusual props and dramatic lighting have been used to create some remarkable black-and-white and color examples of photographic art.

Couture group of the New York Dress Institute, 1957. *Courtesy of the National Archives*

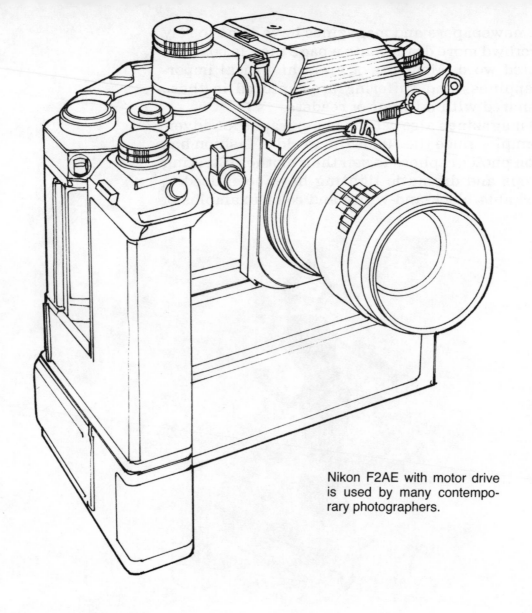

Nikon F2AE with motor drive
is used by many contempo-
rary photographers.

Jerry N. Uelsmann. *Untitled*, 1969.

Photography is always being used in new ways to create expressive personal works of art. No longer concerned with creating photographs that look like paintings, some photographers do create symbolic photographs however. Jerry N. Uelsmann, for example, manipulates negatives in his darkroom in much the same way that Rejlander did over a century ago. Uelsmann, however, is using multiple images taken with a camera to create his own fantasy world in his photographs.

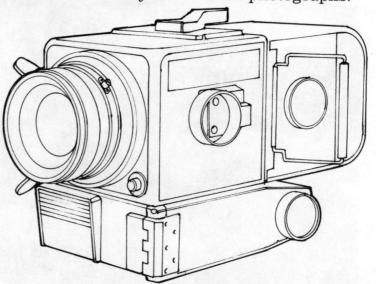

Hasselblad 500 EL. Developed in collaboration with NASA to take photographs on the moon.

Ultimately, the excitement and joy of photography lies in its ability to help us discover and better understand the world in which we live. It also provides us with a means to express our feelings about ourselves and that world, and to look at it in ways that we have never seen it before.

NASA. *The Earth from Lunar Orbit.* Apollo 8, 1968.